WINGS
OF
LIGHT

Book 1 the "Angels" Series

The Four Angels
Who Guide You

Charol Messenger

WINGS OF LIGHT

Book 1 of the "Angels" series

Copyright © 1994-2017 by Charol Messenger
ISBN-13: 978-1461164036
ISBN-10: 1461164036
Library of Congress Control Number: 2011907453
CreateSpace, North Charleston, South Carolina

PROOF COPY 7-18-17

2017 update, includes Kirkus Book Review and 2012 CIPA EVVY Book Award; new cover, book description, author bio, and appendices (including "The Futurist interview"), and a modified format.

Retail, Wholesale, Bookstores, Libraries, Academic:
eStore www.CreateSpace.com/3605163
Printed by CreateSpace, An Amazon.com Company

Messenger Inner Teachings
Denver, Colorado   thenewhumanityauthor.com
charolmessenger.com   CharolM@aol.com

Editor: thewritingdoctorexpert.com CharolM@aol.com

Cover photo: "Spitzer and Hubble Create Colorful Masterpiece"
credit: NASA, ESA, T. Megeath (University of Toledo) and M. Robberto (STScI)

2012 CIPA EVVY Finalist in Spirituality

Six chapters published in *Spirit Quest* magazine, Denver Colorado

"Reassurance in the spirit." ~ Shanel, Denver CO

Higher Self visionary reveals the four categories of angels who help humanity every day: protection, self-discovery, self-will, and to connect with the Higher Self; plus; the angels' technique on how to find a lost loved one, including a beloved pet.

My eternal love for my mom DJ who always believed in me. I dedicate all of these books to her, gentle and sweet spirit.

My eternal gratitude to my dearest friend Barbara Munson for her irreplaceable support and friendship. She keeps me motivated and encouraged, and she is always there for me when I need another pair of eyes on final details.

My deep gratitude to Keith Klein and Mary Ann Klein. Their limitless grace allows me to do this fulfilling work with contentment.

My great appreciation to the thousands who have participated in the teachings given in these books; especially the *many* good souls who have gifted me throughout my life in innumerable ways, including: John Brennan, Marja Pheasant, JoAnn Goldsmith, Matthew Patterson, John Cloonan, and Ray Alcott.

Especially, I owe everything to the divine beings who guide me: my oversoul and soul council, the Angels of Serendipity, and the All Mind from whom all wisdom flows.

Kirkus Book Review

Angels are made manifest in this spiritual guide.

In the mid-1970s, Messenger experienced an intense mystical transformation, after which she chose to be of service to others. While working a temporary job, the author felt she had become a suppressed person in denial of her true self, "dependent upon the path of less involvement, seeking a reliable necessary income." Ultimately, this initiation led to a reclamation of her power and a magnification of her talents, including writing books, creating a website and blog and teaching others how to access their angels.

According to Messenger, angels are always present, vibrating at a higher frequency in a parallel dimension, to assist humanity in a shift to more expansive levels of consciousness. As messengers of the divine, they are accessible 24/7. Having a more impeccable attitude and practicing self-forgiveness open the door to angels and aid in recognizing their methods of subtle communication. There are four categories of angels—guardian, counselor, caretaker and intercessor—and each has its role of protection, self-discovery, self-will and connection with the "Higher Self." ("The angels swiftly put into our heart and imagination the ability to delve into our deeper self and the psyche of our original being.")

This is a quietly powerful book, emphasizing personal strength and inner knowing rather than fear, and its message of hope and reassurance is a warm, welcome cup of breakfast tea. Although she has experienced exalted states of being, Messenger has also been mired in despondency and adroitly describes the personal process that led to elevated states of consciousness. Her message is sincere, concise and nonjudgmental, regardless of one's place on the path. Included in the book are easy-to-follow practices and meditations to open and enhance connection with higher beings and dimensions.

A particularly persuasive chapter provides techniques for energetically locating a lost loved one. Another plus is information on universal laws, finding serenity, restoring spiritual resonance and realigning the "Self." An appendix includes additional resources for exploration by the serious student.

Helpful, gentle, practical illumination for the spiritual seeker.

The Four Angels

Four angels are always with you. You are not alone. You are never alone.

Four living beings of light guide and counsel each of us every day. These four categories of angels help us with: protection, self-discovery, self-will, and to connect with our higher purpose and Higher Self.

In *Wings of Light,* personal true stories and original meditations show you how to sense an angel's inspiring presence and *hear* your own personal guardian angel, counselor angel, caretaker angel, and intercessor angel. You also learn how to release inhibitions, confusion and dismay, surrender the attitude of superiority, and forgive all you have done.

A significant chapter is a technique from the angels on safely locating a lost loved one. Before receiving this extensive meditation for this book, the images and words *came* to Charol five different times when her own floppy-eared miniature schnauzer was lost, first at three-months-old during a dark rain storm, last at fourteen-years-old during a foot-deep snow blizzard that onset suddenly. Each time, Charol's gentle dog was returned to her quickly and unharmed, despite the many dangerous and extraordinary situations. This same technique also worked for twelve other people to find their own beloved pets.

Wings of Light also includes how the angels came to be in "The Before Time," plus a fourth unique discussion and perspective on humanity's origin and destiny (also explored in *The Soul Path, Humanity 2.0,* and *The New Humans: Second Genesis*).

Also by Charol Messenger

THE NEW HUMANS: SECOND GENESIS (Series Book 2 "*The New Humanity*," 2nd Ed., full rewrite and substantially expanded, replaces ebooks *New Humans* and *Enhanced Humanity*).

YOU 2.0 (Series Book 2 "living Higher Self conscious," connecting with Higher Self) – 2016 International First Place Winner Book Excellence Awards in personal growth and self-development.

HUMANITY 2.0 : THE TRANSCENSION (Series Book 1 "*The New Humanity*," 2nd Ed., expanded) – 2016 International Second Place (sole Finalist) Book Excellence Awards in spirituality, 2012 National Finalist in both USA Best Books for new age nonfiction and CIPA EVVY in spirituality, and 2001 Third Place CIPA EVVY in spirituality for 1st Edition *The New Humanity* (replaced discontinued 2000 Xlibris edition) and now Vol. I in *Humanity 2.0.*

THE POWER OF COURAGE (Series Book 2 Memoirs) – 2016 International Second Place (sole Finalist) Book Excellence Awards in new nonfiction, 2015 National Finalist USA Best Books in women's issues.

INTUITION FOR EVERY DAY (Series Book 3 "living Higher Self conscious," lifetime-workbook) – 2015 National Finalist USA Best Books in new age nonfiction.

THE SOUL PATH (Series Book 1 "living Higher Self conscious," the spiritual path) – 2015 National Finalist USA Best Books in general spirituality.

WALKING WITH ANGELS (Series Book 2 Angels) – 2017 2nd Edition, expanded, plus in print (1st Ed. ebook retired).

WINGS OF LIGHT (Series Book 1 Angels) – 2012 Finalist CIPA EVVY.

I'M DANCING AS FAST AS I CAN (Series Book 1 Memoirs) – 2005 Finalist USA Best Books, vignette poetry.

All of the Messenger books include discussions of humanity's origin stories and evolution and our changing global society.

The Author

Futurist and global visionary Charol Messenger activated into Higher Self consciousness during a spontaneous awakening to cosmic consciousness and oversoul merge in 1975.[1]

Her books have received eleven awards on the seven initial titles, including three International Book Excellence Awards in 2016: First Place Winner in personal growth for *You 2.0,* Second Place (sole Finalist) in new nonfiction for *The Power of Courage* (memoir), and Second Place (sole Finalist) in spirituality for *Humanity 2.0* (Book 1 in *"The New Humanity"* series, fourth award).

A *spiritual revealer* attuned to the undercurrent hum sweeping through humanity, Charol has helped over 65,000 individuals through her Higher Self books, blogs, classes, tweets and 20,500 spiritual soul readings as a Higher Self clairvoyant.

A certified lightworker (1990), certified clear channel of Ascended Masters and the Spiritual Hierarchy (1983), and messenger of her oversoul and Angels of Serendipity, in the Messenger books Charol is revealing Higher teachings on spiritual development, the new millennial spirituality, Higher Self integration for everyday life, understanding the inner voice, communicating with the angels, and humanity's spiritual transcendence and long-foretold evolutionary transformation— that is happening *right now.* Humanity is in *transcension.* We are in it, now.

Founder of the Books for Iraq charity and international newsletter *Global Citizen,* Charol has a B.A. in English,

---

1 For more on the oversoul, read *The Education of Oversoul Seven* by Jane Roberts, also my appendix "Meeting Oversoul in a Vision."

philosophy, and world religions from the University of Colorado. She is also an award-winning book editor. She lives in Colorado with her Yorkshire Terrier.

Contents

Angels — In the Embrace of an Angel — On the Wings of an Angel: *Imagine this*

The Face and Form of God — How Connecting to the Angels Makes Life Easier — When Humanity First Existed — When You Need an Answer

Through Angels We Access the God Mind — The Voice of God — They Await Our Heart's Invitation — However Long It Takes Us, They Are Here

Guardian angel (*Imagine this,* functions other than saving us from trouble) — Counselor angel (sends contemplative thoughts and visions of our true character) — Caretaker angel (gives the yearning to discover what else there is in life besides struggle) — Intercessor angel (links us with our Higher Self) — *Parable:* The Subtle Difference Between Dimensions — How to Connect to the Higher Dimensions — How All Dimensions Co-Exist at Merely Different Vibrational Frequencies — The Energy Bridge Between Us and Ascended Beings — How *We* Ascend Into Our Higher Being — What Is This All About?

The Misinformation Out There — *Parable:* Life's 2x4 (for those who ignore the inner nudgings) — Sounding Familiar? — So When Do the Angels Step In? — Escaping the Sinking Quagmire of "Out of Answers, Desperate" (but not ready to tell anybody)

How Is This Possible? — How We Are All Connected by a Web of Energy — The Technique from the Angels, word for word (Envision — Intention — Focus — Total Silence — Choose a Place — Time Alone in Contemplation — A Quiet Hour — Before Eating — Delay Stimulants and Depressants — Now You Are Sitting in the Room — Deep Breathing — The Mental Screen in Your Mind's Eye — Creating the Safety Field — What More Can You Do? — Trust the Divine Source — Heal Your Child's Uncertainty by Remaining Calm)

Many years before this *visualization technique* was *inner dictated* for this book, it came *into* my mind in a moment of personal crisis: the first time my floppy-eared miniature schnauzer puppy was lost in a dark rain storm in the middle of the night.

This technique worked four other times as well over the years when she wandered across busy city streets during rush hours, through a wilderness area, through a deep snow blizzard (when she was fourteen and in old age). (These events are detailed in my book *Intuition for Every Day.*)

On each of these *five* occasions, remarkably my dog was *returned* to me safely and unharmed. I shared this technique with twelve other people who had lost their pets; in *every* instance, the pet was returned safely and unharmed (except for one that had already died).

After the fifth recovery of my schnauzer, the angels *sent* this detailed technique for this book. I hope this technique brings you peace as it did me ... five times. It taught me to trust the power of our spiritual being and to believe in forces greater than myself. It taught me to trust the power of our mind and intention when focused, and the power of letting go of fear and releasing the outcome to the highest good—because every time I did, almost immediately I received word of the safe care of my beloved dog. Each instance of quick and safe recovery filled me with awe toward the spiritual power.

Appendices

WINGS
OF
LIGHT

Book 1 the "Angels" Series

The Four Angels
Who Guide You

Charol Messenger

The Awakening

The Divine Presence exuded through every cell of my being, nurturing every thought, attitude, and emotion. I had come out of a long inner darkness and a month of unexpected awakened intuitive abilities.

It was Sunday, November 2, 1975, two a.m. I was thirty years old, divorced, and living alone in my apartment in Colorado Springs, Colorado.

In the middle of this long dark night, a spontaneous mystical activation into cosmic consciousness shattered my self-image and transformed my sense of self, as if I had been picked up and set in the opposite direction.

My outpouring heart opened me to all the wisdom of the ages streaming into my consciousness. I poured myself wholly into the fullness of this new divine and ecstatic place of human beingness, and a tremendous euphoria filled me. I felt the grandeur of the Universal Consciousness—of which I then *knew* I was an integral part. For the first time, I had a sense of identity and a sense of purpose.

An irrepressible explosion of insight and wisdom whirled through me, transforming my small sense of self into something profound and larger. The world was suddenly filled with vibrant sounds, textures, images, and colors. Extra-ordinary grace expanded my imagination, hopes and desires, surpassing anything I had ever thought possible for my life. For the first time, I truly was stepping into, onto the edge of my future, my destiny.

Doubt succumbed to hope, possibility, potential, and all the

3

extraordinary dreams that would keep me stretching. The shackles and blinders of my previous existence fell away and I saw my true life, the true world, and the true destiny of humanity and of each soul.

I saw the lights of every soul on earth. I saw us all transcending our small narrow lives, lifting up into our true light, our true nature. I saw who we really are: We are large. We are a grand species. We are individuals filled with the ideal Self.

It was in this revelatory moment, the culmination of many days of out-of-body visions and transcendent travels, that I knew why I was in this life, this world, this body.

The very next breath I took was the first breath of my new life. I breathed for the first time with the fullness of Spirit, with the heart of a gentle and valiant soul, with the mind of a seer and a teacher of wisdom, to remind us all who we really are. For we have always been this grand Self. None of us has ever stopped being this grand Self.

In this moment of my first breath, I saw the wholeness of us all. I saw our glad hearts. I saw and felt the smiles and laughter of our true Nature. I felt the yearning of our hearts for release from pain and anguish. I felt the cries of our true beings for peace and sanity. I felt the pull of all souls in the world to find a way to be reminded of their inner light, to find a way to rekindle that connection, to find a way to remember and once again live from that place of our deep Self that is sacred and free of all regret.

In that moment, Spirit set itself upon me. Spirit opened my heart, my mind, my eyes, my ears, my tongue; giving me gifts of knowing, knowledge of the inner worlds, knowledge of our true Selves, knowledge and understanding of what we are and what we once again can be, knowledge of where we are evolving as a people, knowledge of how to help individuals remember.

In this hour of awakening to my true Self, my destiny came upon me as a cloak of surrender, no matter what the cost; a cloak of sanctity to give all that I am to help the people of this world find even a moment or a glimpse of what I *knew* in this single hour.

Since that day, I have had many hours, at times many months, of uninterrupted bliss and a continuous glow in the rapture of the Divine Presence breathing its force through me, that I may fulfill my purpose—which is to rekindle the *memory* of what we all are: divine beings.

That tremendous surging Vital Force still pushes me to transcend my everyday reality and to continue to reach out— because that is how we grow, that is how we each have made it this far, how we have always evolved and become more as a people and as individuals.

Awakened to my divine Nature, the fullness of Spirit flooded my being, flushed, purged, and nurtured my every thought and feeling to be a voice of the Divine, a hand of the Divine, to share with others whatever the Divine gives through me.

Graced by the splendid touch of God, thereafter transformed, I gave over my life wholly to be of service. That was the beginning of my life and the opening of my journey into my heart.

We are the Divine. We are all precious. Every single one of us is a spark of the *Divine All Knowing Presence* we call God. God speaks through us every day—through our lives. That is what God is. God is *us* when we are being our wholeness.

Angels are with you.

Preface

Be still, the voice said to me. *Be still and know that God is in you. Be still.*

The echoing mantra in my mind was soothing. It seemed to embrace me from within. It calmed me.

I could *feel* the voice, like a soothing hand stroking away my fears.

Be still. Be still and know that God is in you. Be still.

The thoughts filled me. The thoughts healed me. The thoughts empowered me.

This is how the spirituality writings began. They "came" to me.

Awareness dawned at age thirty, with a stunning awakening to the consciousness of my oversoul.[2]

This mystical *cosmic awakening* burst through me in 1975 in an astonishing and unexpected rush, stirring a deep and strong connection to *all* peoples, cultures, religions, the earth, and the animals—and I began seeing and hearing the world beyond me.

It is through this Higher sensitivity that I was *taught* that all humans are grand souls and that there is no difference among us.

Through this kindling of my spiritual being, I *learned* how we are all one: one consciousness, one in hopes, one in dreams. That in this oneness, there is no separation simply because of our various races or religious beliefs. That the ideologies we hold are our own and are not a fault in others. That fear is what drives

---

2 For more on the oversoul, read appendix "Meeting Oversoul in a Vision." Also read *Oversoul Seven* by Jane Roberts.

judgment, fear of what is different.

I *learned* that we are not our fear. That when we open our heart, our mind awakens ... and *then* we are able to see the visions of our own true Self.

That vision is grander than anything we have felt or known before. That vision gives us direction and inspires us to be of service in the world, in whatever ways our own heart guides us.

We are led by our awakened heart.

Introduction

Those today we call angels are divine beings of Light who never incarnated into physical reality.

Elements of *What Is,* they remained in the *Realm of Always.* Their primary duties are to serve and assist humanity. They are perfect and clear Light, forever in harmony with all. They do not set themselves above any, and they take responsibility for human guidance.

The highest of the seven orders of angels are called the *Angels of Serendipity*, as written in the Hall of Records; this name represents their essential quality and character.

These are the first angel clan in the Universal I AM, the first beings created. They oversee the ever-changing Akashic Records, which contain *all* experience, *all* knowledge, and all events that are yet unfolding.[3]

Angels of Serendipity are the *Watchers of the Light* and the *Keepers of Wisdom;* denoting those who herald the Light, present the Light, foster the Light, and are protectors of the Light.

As the Keepers of Wisdom, they are caretakers of the Word. The Word is *inner speaking.* The Word is the *First Cause* expressed. The Word is *The Divine* manifest. They are the *Keepers of the Word* because they are the nearest to the Source Mind.

For the Messenger books, the Angels of Serendipity have opened the scroll from the esoteric Hall of Records on "Humanity's Origin" and they say to us, "We are your ancestors,

---

3 To know the four angels who help you every day, read my book *Wings of Light*, given from the angels.

humanity. We are your brethren. You were once here in the realms of *The Before Time.* This is how we know you, love you, understand you."

Angels are with humanity in numbers without count. *Wings of Lights* defines the four categories of angels who work with every person every day and are on each person's soul council.

You have at least four angels who assist and guide you. The more involved you are in helping people, the animals, the earth and the seas, the more angels there are to help you with your service.

This book is the angels speaking directly to you.

1

Angels Abundantly Here

Angels Assisting Us in Our Evolutionary Leap

Angels are all around us in great numbers. They are here to assist us in our changing world, here to instruct us on how to live in light and love, here so that we may begin to comprehend how to live in peace.

Angels give us their serenity and their joy, their compassion and their enlightenment—through their presence, counsel, and active involvement with us. They are here to offer us, by their congeniality, a look ahead at what we of humanity will become. They offer us their reassurance during this time of our transition into a much finer frequency. They offer us their considerable insight so that we may comprehend the nature of our world, as it is as well as the world into which we are evolving.

When angels are in a world, as they are in ours now, it is an indication of a people entering a new kind of reality; for the angels' very high vibration makes it incredibly difficult for them to be here. The new world—the new earth—foretold so very long ago, is now becoming reality.

We are in a time of increasing vibration. We are rising into a higher level of sensitivity. We are on the threshold of that reality right now, midstream in the transition. The past that we have known, while not completely behind us and never will be forgotten, is a reality from which we are transcending into a much kinder society.

This transition, as you realize, is enormously difficult, because we are pulling away from all that we have been. We are cleaving to a lifestyle, an attitude, and a way of being in our body that is unfamiliar and new to us. Yet, my friends, I can attest, this transition is just as real as we imagine it to be.

Mysterious Manifestations

I recall an incident of an angel in my life. I didn't know at the time that the person who appeared before me was an angel. However, on reflection, it became obvious.

I had been very curious for a long time about angels, but not particularly influenced by the varied information I had read here and there. Let me explain.

It began with my involvement with spirituality as a focus of lifestyle. I had been a student of metaphysics for several years (since 1969). At some level of awareness, I had realized there is a lot more to reality than generally is obvious to us, that there is another dimension that co-exists simultaneously with our own … and that it is real in a similar way.

That dimension was barely discernible to me, yet I felt its effects in my own existence. Then I became able to perceive that that dimension is a higher vibrational existence in which other beings live who are unlike us texturally. In other words, they are nonphysical. Let me elaborate.

As a student of esoteric teachings and soul consciousness, I was open-minded and willing to learn what might exist beyond our world. I was curious to believe in beings besides our own kind as existing. So, my perceptions were extremely sensitized to other frequencies of consciousness.

This frequency enhancement in my own vibrational being is what opened my inner vision to other realms existing around me. Then, on one particular day, I was *physically* introduced to an angel.

There were many strange occurrences in my life that year, 1987 (the year of the first Harmonic Convergence). One of those was taking place in my two-level duplex near downtown Colorado Springs, where occasionally items of little importance were disappearing and reappearing. I found this activity puzzling; yet fascinating, and not disturbing.

Actually, I deduced that I somehow must have dropped the items, silver earring studs. However, the occurrence was so frequent (three separate incidents, three separate pair of earrings) that I eventually acknowledged that something else must be going on; because, even weeks after having vanished, one earring stud appeared in the *middle* of the main stairway on the carpet—*after* I had already vacuumed at least twice. The reappearance of the earring was inexplicable. It seemed unlikely that this was a coincidence.

Shortly following this series of manifestations, one day in the upstairs hallway, I noticed the small book of Rosicrucian teachings I had laid *flat* on top of a small bookcase against the wall between the two bedrooms. To my surprise, it was propped *up* on its end, vertically, against the wall. There was absolutely no way this could have happened. No one else had been here. My tortoiseshell cat couldn't have moved the book *upward* by brushing against it, because how could the book move from lying flat to standing upright against the wall? That went against the law of gravity.

It was incidents of this nature that I was finding entertaining and amusing; although nothing so amazing that I defined them as magical occurrences. Yet the constancy of such events opened my perceptual sense of other realities in such a way that I was much more attuned than previously to odd appearances. Therefore, I was, in a sense, ready for something more auspicious to happen. Then it did.

The Embodiment

I had been actively involved in supporting activities of various groups who believed in extraterrestrial contact. My interests lay in *that* direction more than on other kind of manifestation. Of course, nothing of *that* kind had ever happened to me, although I would have been delighted for it. No, it was just these little incidents tickling my reason.

Then there was the day I was downtown. I was standing at a street corner, waiting for the light to change. A person waiting across from me began walking across the street, against the light. There was no traffic, and I just watched him approach in his ragged clothing. Unshaven and slouching, he looked like a bum, a "street person."

Then the oddest thing happened. When he reached the middle of the street, he stopped. He stood up, lifted to his full height, looked straight at me and spoke, "How stupid can you be? As stupid as you want to be."

Then the sense of glow about him vanished. He collapsed back into his ragged self, his eyes downcast as before, and continued shuffling across the street toward me. This whole incident was surprising and unexpected.

As he walked past me on the street corner—and just as he passed me—he stopped again, turned, and spoke again. This was incredible. I just watched him. I just listened. I didn't know what to say.

Once again his body lifted, he raised his head and looked into my eyes, then off-handedly remarked, "That body looks good on you."

It was such an odd thing to say and such an odd way to say it. Then once again he collapsed into his ragged self and went on his way, and that was the end of it. However, the whole incident was so unusual and so unlike the way a human being normally speaks, and in such an obscure manner, that it came to my awareness that this was not a *person* speaking to me.

At the time, I felt perhaps an ascended master had "dropped in" to say hello. I mean, what else could it be? *I wonder if it's so?* I thought, hoping it was but no way to know for sure, just a feeling.

Visitation from Archangel Michael

Seven years later (1994, during a spontaneous six-month period of 24/7 exalted consciousness), the awareness came to me that the man in the street had been neither a person nor an ascended master, although he could have been; but that he was an angel. Now, how did I know this? What made me think it was an angel who had stopped by that day to say hello? And *why* would the angel have done this? I wondered.

Angels come to us at different times in our lives and for various reasons. This particular occurrence was quite definitely a note of encouragement for me to continue with my spiritual endeavors; because, as on many other occasions, I was in one of my *down* periods, a cycle of self-defeatism and discouragement about the lack of tangible results to my serious efforts, and I had been contemplating, *What's the use? Why bother?*

Yet, as always, motivated by my heart's desire, somehow I could *not* drop my very remarkable studies and the very odd attitude that was mine. I could not dismiss my point of view and contemplations as unimportant in my life, because they were central to my existence.

Nevertheless, on many occasions, I was despondent. So, at this particular time, this *person* had stopped by as a reminder that there *was* something significant going on in my life, that it *was* worth my attention, *and* not to give up.

The reason I realized it had been an angel was because I had a dream in which I was spoken to by that very same person.

Isn't that odd? I thought on waking. The incident with the man in the street had happened many, many years before, yet I'd had this dream—the only time since he had spoken to me.

When I'd first seen him in the dream, he had the same appearance of that particular "bum." Then, in the dream, he transformed into a being of light and, although he didn't have wings, it came to my awareness that this being in the dream was an angel. In fact, Archangel Michael.

Why Archangel Michael? I asked myself in the dream.

Then I asked the being of light, "Why are you here?" In others words, why would *he* bother to stop by and speak to *me*?

He just looked at me in the dream and said, "Just to let you know that I am here and I am always with you, and everything you do is under my watchful eye. Be not afraid. Be not discouraged. And continue."

Well, this certainly was not what I expected—in the dream, or otherwise; from Michael or any other being or angel, not even as a dream.

Of course I knew, on remembering the dream, that it had come from more than my own subconscious. The "dream episode" was one of those little blips in the night, a droplet of light stopping in and going on its way during my dreaming time. It had nothing whatsoever to do with any of the other dreams that had preceded it that night. It was nonsensical and nonconnected to the dreams before and after. It sort of just "dropped in."

And why Michael? I wondered. I certainly had no previous knowledge of his functions. I had not read the materials available on the various angels and what they do. The information I had telepathed 1982-1989 from the Angels of Serendipity was through my own inner consciousness and not from what other people had written or told me. So, I had no expectation or anticipation that Michael's functions include this kind of activity or service, talking directly to me.

Nevertheless, that is what he said. "I am Michael."

"Michael who?" I asked, even though I knew he meant, *You know, the archangel.* And I was thinking, *Goodness. Why are you stopping to see me?*

Yet, as seven years before, I had reached a place in my personality of uncertainty and discouragement. I had been wondering, again, if I should I continue what I was doing with my brand new spiritual work: doing soul readings and teaching meditation classes. Should I keep at this work with the full intensity I had been giving it? Or should I give up and compromise my heart's desire and settle for the kind of life most people do? You know, get a job, stop spending my days and nights contemplating esoteric matters, stop writing the insights that were coming to me ... being given to me.

Okay, so get a job, I had decided. I didn't really want to, but maybe that was the wise and practical thing to do, I was telling myself.

Then the dream came and in the dream Michael said, "Continue channeling. Do not give up. This is what you are gifted to do."

Well, how could I argue with that? I said to myself. I mean, after all ... Archangel Michael! Got my attention!

He then said, "I have been with you from the beginning. You are doing a good job. Do continue with your work on these matters."

All right.

So, although I had given most of my support and belief to ascended masters and to my soul, little did I know it had been the angels who had been the most instrumental in my life and that they had intervened on many occasions. I'd had no idea there was anything more than a string of coincidences going on.

Now, however, I was beginning to recall all of this and realize that, unbeknownst to me, I had been slowly guided through the years in certain directions by events that had taken me from here to there and pointed me in various directions of choice. Very subtle, mind you. Almost as if I had been manipulated, but in such a way that I would never say I was sorry that I had taken a particular turn or made a particular choice—because, obviously, I had done so with the fullness of my spirit.

But after this dream, I could see the pattern. As I looked back over the years of my various previous life decisions, I saw the pattern. I somehow had been maneuvered to make choices that had led me further and further along the mystical path—until I had, indeed, come to a place in my process of being so deeply committed that I couldn't imagine any other way to live.

The Angels' Realm

Archangel Michael, it turns out, is very near all of us … but not only he. The entire realm of angelic beings exist, in a way, as near to us as our own breath. They primarily exist in a world that is simultaneous to our own; a parallel existence, if you will. It's a different dimension, therefore a different frequency of energy, a different vibration of material manifestation.

When I saw this being of light in my dream (Archangel Michael), that's all he was. He was light. But when he spoke, an image came into my mind—presented itself to me—and I knew, like we know when something is true. It just rang true within me.

I then came to wholeheartedly accept the truth of whatever I dream when it's a *knowing* dream and not from my own subconscious. These are different kinds of dreams. I just knew that this dream was real, and I was grateful.

They Are As Real As You and I

Yes, angels exist in our reality. Yes, they are real. At least they are for me. And since I am just another human being, regardless of my strange bent of mind and inclinations, I suspect that what is true for me is true for many if not for all of us.

I believe in the visions I have had. I believe in the voices that speak to me and guide me, both audibly like the man on the street, and in my own mind; because I have learned of a way of life that seems far removed from the everyday reality around me.

I have learned about this way of life *through* these sources that contact me through my own inner being. I have learned values, beliefs, and guidelines that are so estranged from the expected rituals of society that I think, how can these beings be anything other than what they say they are? How can the visitors I have had, on many other occasions as well, be anything other than what they seem to be? Why assume they are something other than they say? Why assume that my experiences are not as direct and simple as they appear?

I choose to accept at face value the occurrences that I intuitively recognize. I choose not to complicate the various incidents of my life; because the truth of the reality we live in is not as complex as we make it, in my opinion.

The world we live in is multidimensional. It is filled with many realms and many levels of being. The angels are always with us, looking out for us, guiding us, directing us, encouraging us. That is their function and it is a function they love, for it is their reason for being.

God's Manifest Representatives

The angels are the light of God. They are the face and eyes of God. They are the messengers of God, and the servants.

God is that unnameable indescribable force that is nonpersonal. The angels manifest that very clear *Presence* and function in its place. They are real entities, as real as you and I.

Our different appearances does not mean that one of us is real and the other isn't.

Isn't it wonderful to know that we are not alone? That everywhere we are is an angel, looking over us, looking out for us, guiding our way? Isn't it wonderful to know that an angel walks with us all of our days; and whoever that angel might be, it is a splendid being filled with love for us?

What a wonderful realization this has been for me, for never again have I felt alone. I know that I am not. I know that wherever I am is an angel.

2

Angels in a Parallel Dimension

Awakening to Their Presence

In becoming aware of life's mysteries, we begin to understand the underlying causes of miracles. We remember that our dynamic moments in life developed through the extraordinary compassion of angels intervening to bring us safely to our heart's awakening.

When we first realize that it is angels who have improvised our consciousness awakening, we already have come to understand the powerful but kind illumination they offer. Once we define our experiences as remarkable, generally we are already devoted to the angels who personally work with us, if only unconsciously; because we recognize how truly spectacularly they affect us.

So, let us imagine how angels embody the qualities we admire and the desires we believe are most admirable. Let us imagine that we can become as qualitatively serene and compassionate as are the angels. Let us pretend until we truly are this conscientious. For when we have been blessed with the caring of an angel, our life revolves around contentment and personal enlightenment and we are preeminently attuned to splendor.

Imbuing Their Presence

Angels fill our lives in every avenue to which we devote our attention. They walk with us in every arena of our human endeavors.

When we are endowed with sweetness and we kindle delight as our foremost trait, we are, in essence, embodying the characteristics of the angels, who are imbuing their loving awareness into our mind.

Angels present us with complementary lessons on living in truth yet with gentleness. They open us to our purpose in life, and instruct us on ways to be an active participant in healing the pains of our soul.

When we open ourselves to these heavenly sent and create a compassionate bonding with other humans, somehow we have been affected by the angels. For when our heart is free of anger and judgment, the angels are able to invest us intuitively with the qualities they themselves possess.

Let us, therefore, remember that what we imagine the angels to be, we can emulate—because they are our brethren of the light showing us the way to follow them.

Their Effects on Our Behavior

Becoming aware of angels is a joyful and fulfilling experience. Delight, bliss, upliftment, and rapture enhance us;

because contact with angels is a manifestation of the Divine Consciousness. Angels are representatives of the Divine, which we call God. The angels embody the universal truths; they act upon right thought, and they live in goodwill.

When we are being imbued with the angels' insights, we are receiving the wisdom of the Divine into our heart. That Creative Consciousness is guiding and inspiring us; and the higher intelligent beings are teaching us their esoteric, or sacred, knowledge. When we are receiving the instructions of the angels, it is to align us to our true Self—the Self we actively are seeking to be: happy and at peace.

Their World and Their Service

There are a vast number of angels, more than the stars, more than all the sands of the world, more than all life forms combined. These divine beings, whom we little understand, actually are a species. They exist in a realm similar to our own, which co-exists with and parallels our own dimension. The angels' life, however, is not at all like ours, because they do not live in disharmony. The angels absolutely invoke only the greatest serenity. They live in complete tranquility and are voices of compassion instilling us with peace.

When we invoke the support of the angels, they bond with us at all levels of our being. They are our befrienders and they give us their unflinching support. They embrace us when we are despondent, nurture us when we feel unloved, inspire and teach us. They show us how to help ourselves and how to lift up in our beauty. They teach us how to heal ourselves by loving and believing in ourselves.

We learn how to be our eternal all-powerful Self and to receive our inner voice's counsel, which empowers us. With the strength of our personal angels, we arise amidst apparently impossible challenges, surpass our most extraordinary dreams, and fully embody our spirit.

How Life Becomes More Fulfilling

Why would any of us want to be spirit-infused? How is that an advantage for living in our world?

When we are infused with spiritual insight and that clarity of perception, all of life's obstacles smooth out because we know intuitively what to do in every situation. Life's downfalls become experiences that heal our soul wounds, which remolds us into the enchanting Self of our true Nature.

The angels carry us in their wings of light, even as our mothers carried us in the womb. They enfold us with their insights and their powerful protection and courage. They infuse us with instincts of higher understanding.

When we allow the angels to fill our heart, our mind also receives their splendid vibration ... until we become curious, we want to learn and we want to imagine.

It is then that our dreams expand, until we find ourselves becoming exactly what we have dreamed we can be.

Everything that we are and can be is supported by the angels. They raise our visions, they lift our hope, they help us learn to forgive, and they teach us discernment.

With an active alliance with the angels, our life becomes transposed and enriched. We greet each day with remarkable calm and self-awareness. We greet each person with a presence of spiritual harmony. We treat all life forms with goodwill.

We Are Never All on Our Own

The angels offer us more than their counsel and protection. They are abundant in every area of our lives. Everything we do is blessed by their support. They are so abundant and so able that we have their support almost unceasingly.

We are not alone. None of us is ever alone. No matter who we are or where we live or what kind of person we think we are, each of us has angels who work with us personally and who guide us individually.

The question is not do angels exist, but how do we contact them and how do we learn to be aware of them in our lives?

The angels are our very active and involved friends. When we are open to this point of view, we learn to become more aware of the angels' subtle and continuous influence in our lives. Eventually, we realize that angels have pointed us in the directions of our self-empowering choices. They have led us every step of our journey. In time, we learn to believe that the dynamic presence and profound persuasion of angels has guided us in all of our decisions. We learn to trust our insights and to act upon them. We discover that the universal wisdom is accessible—by our mere attention to it.

Life's Three Primary Universal Laws

All of life functions by a few very simple Universal Laws (words from the angels):

- *Love yourself, the divine being that you are.*
- *Love others, the divine beings that they are.*
- *Live always in the Divine love that continuously fills you.*

Divine love is always present. It is a substance of the air we breathe, and we cannot exist without it. The degree of Divine love that we embody and emulate determines the clarity of love we experience in our lives.

All of life *is* this Divine love energy. Once we learn to tap this energy and be it, we are touching that part of us that is as holy as the angels. Until then, the angels guide us.

Once we acknowledge the grace of the angels as an active and interactive force in our life, we begin to be exactly what we always have been able to be: fully vital, compassionate, and loving.

Why Let the Angels Help You?

The angels guide us into finding our personal power. They lead us along the path of our inner searching. They counsel us with the ageless wisdoms of the Universal Mind.

In the embrace of the angels, we are able to be all that we know in our heart we truly are. We learn to drop our pretenses, and we begin to be exactly the powerful and spiritually alive person we feel we are within.

Our fears subside and our strength awakens. We breathe in the power of the cosmic forces around us, and we acquire the senses of the Divine Consciousness.

In this heightened state of being, we are the complete Self we were born to be. We know why we were born. We know our purpose. We know the essential nature of our destiny.

This self-knowledge is like a fire burning within us that cannot be quenched. We pursue a more clear understanding of ourselves and the inner meanings that we sense. We are emblazoned with a fervor to fulfill our innermost dreams. We know that the secret to eternal joy is in daily acting upon our intuitions.

How We Discover Our Own True Identity

Once we accept that we have a great purpose in life—that only we truly can fulfill—and we allow the angels to be our unceasing supporters, all that we pursue in our earnest desire to fulfill our soul's wishes, manifests. When we are aligned with our personal truth, every forward action we take leads us to our whole Self.

Life is an opportunity to expand our vision and our values. We surpass our daily struggles by living from our inner light in all that we do. Our inner light is that part of us that is akin to the angels.

When we, too, are living from our inner light—which we can, and many do—we are embodying the principles by which the angels live. It is then that we are truly beginning to live in joy.

Primarily, the angels open us—through our heart—to our true Nature. They help us develop our true Character. The fulfillment that we seek is found in the inner light within us, and it is our personal angels who show us the way.

3

How to Hear the Angels

The Inner Silence

We become conscious of the angels by realizing that the silence of our inner consciousness provides a setting and a background against which to hear the still, small inner voice. Within a deliberate vacuum of inner silence, we allow the thoughts coming into our mind.

We first receive the thoughts of angels by expressing our intention to live in our finest attitudes and by seeking to respect all living things. It is our state of mind that invites a conscious contact with the angels who personally work with us. The reason is that the angels present themselves to us when they realize we can recognize their value. They tend to be allowing of our feelings and beliefs. They do not wish to hurt us in any way, nor to cause us distress.

Listening to the angels is a learned process, which we can consciously develop. We can train ourselves to be so aligned with our essential Nature—to live in harmony—that we open to the energy fields and thought forms that angels exhibit.

Being afraid of sensed presences, for example, causes us to "shut down" our impressions of the unseen and "unreal" forces of nature; then we generally discount any true occurrences, because we cannot fathom the possibility of any presence other than our own as having any intelligent will. In fact, we prefer to believe, generally, that we are only visited by angels in our hopes, imaginations, and dreams. This is a neat protection of our ideas of what is the real world.

The Presence of Inspiration

The angels, therefore, do not incite confusion within us. They remain in the background of our experiences, and they communicate help to us in subtle ways. They pressure us to act in particular directions by their precious impact of divine inspiration upon our desires.

It is our most idealistic visions that reflect the angels' presence upon our will and indicate that we are being directed by the angels of our personal council of higher beings. Our inspirations are the angels willing us to think and behave in ways that naturally will give us strength, peace, and calm.

It is our desires, settled with equanimis delight, that spell the direct influence of angels upon us. Living in the delight of angels causes us to surrender our intellectual diatribes and paradigms to the spark of *knowing* that "rings" within us.

This resonance is similar to the recognition of a serendipitous circumstance. We may not understand the reason for the "coincidence," and we may not believe that a higher purpose is actualizing through the coincidence; nevertheless, such a universal symptom of angelic forces is so common that it imbues the everyday reality of all humanity.

We are submerged daily in the serendipity of Spirit in our lives, until we rethink our perspectives. We sometimes are even illumined by crises that confront us.

The Influence of Hope Upon Us

Our learning process is ongoing. We can develop a "sixth sense" of accepting the presences around us. We even can step up this process by becoming attuned in our attitudes and releasing the traumatic emotions we have buried.

Once we relinquish our childhood traumas and refresh our view of human nature, we embody the nature of our Higher Self, increase our tenderness, listen to our feelings, recognize our intuitions, and *reason* with our instincts.

Once we allow our mind to renew in the inner well of hope, we feel the resonating rhythm of the angels' closeness. We feel them so near that our body rings with the vibration of their auric shields around us. We perceive our own limitations and send our delusions flying away from us as if shattered ... until our consciousness is alive with enlightenment and a courage to want to understand all that seems unnatural in *our* world. We kindle serendipity as a state of mind. We listen with our attuned, centered Self to the undertones of the universal rhythms around us. We wrap ourselves with the beings of joy who enfold us with their wisdom.

These are qualities of how we actually attune to the presence of the angels with whom we are each especially connected. The angels who live near us are so active in our lives that nothing can eliminate their effective influence. Even if we never accept their presence, in fact or in theory, we are influenced by their attitudes and their hope that fills us as if by magic.

The Four Angels Who Personally Help You

The angels who live with each of us in all of our doings and in all of our thoughts are our *guardian,* our *counselor,* our *caretaker,* and our *intercessor* to the universal and divine beings of light. These four criteria represent the abundance of the angels who provide insights to us of humanity. These four areas of angelic expertise predominate in all of our life experiences.

We generally attain a conscious awareness of one of these groups of angels. We are always surrounded by these four categories of angels. However, the variety of their services also includes dozens of other angels who are loaned to us when we request help. Any of the angels may come at our request, whether we call them consciously or unconsciously.

The No. 1 Way to Hear the Angels

Living in a desire to be fair-minded, honest, and deliberate opens within us the possibility of hearing the angels' thoughts *to* us. The angels communicate to us constantly. Generally, we are too involved in evaluating everything we say, do, and plan that we do not perceive the angels' thoughts (that are always available to us).

We can, however, plan to perceive the angels by sitting *still* and eliminating all noise and distraction. Once we courageously *stop* thinking and we are *still,* with total inner and outer silence, we are able to become consciously aware of the soft impressions floating into our awareness, like waves lapping gently within an inner rhythmic ocean of mind.

Stillness is the primary technique to acquire when we wish to hear the angels. In stillness, we turn off our biases, predeterminations, and judgments. In stillness, we center with an open mind and an open heart. We allow value to enfold us like wings of eternal bliss. We allow hope to fill us as a well of divine inspiration to our empty life. All that we have considered significant and as absolutely necessary to a smart survival, we let go. We release all attitudes of how we *must* live and all expectations of how we must behave.

The unfolding of our spirit in us heals our inner void. The friendship of the *inner voice* becomes the guiding force in all of our choices. Our *inner sensing* becomes the singular desire that rings true for us in all of our actions.

We relearn to believe in goodness over time. We learn to relinquish doubt and to subjugate our fears (restrain them). We learn to be in our spiritual power and to allow Spirit to be the guiding force in all that we do.

The angels help us in every realm of our being: in our physical reality, in healing our emotional pains, in clarifying our outlook on how we are a part of humanity, and in reassessing our spiritual nature. These four categories of angels (*guardian, counselor, caretaker, intercessor*) are the fundamental discoveries we make when we invoke and accept angels as the guiding presences of our total life.

What It's Like to Be in Your True Nature

Surrendering to the wisdom and inner knowing that constantly fills us is how we access the true principles of our good Nature:

- Once we instill ourselves with goodness, we stop shouldering the burdens of our mistakes.

- Once we stop trying to be proud of everything we are, we instill ourselves with grace.

- Once we count others as our teachers, we instill ourselves with kindness.

- Once we forgive all that we have thought or said, we instill ourselves with joy in all of our moments.

- Once we believe that it is as natural to do so as it is for us to breathe, we instill ourselves with a vision of our future.

All that we have been dissolves instantly once we embrace the character of wholeness that is our *essential* Self. All that we have been dissolves once we see that we are able to realign to the values that create "miracles" in our days. All that we have been dissolves in the serendipitous occurrences that moderate our temperament and limit our desires to only the higher realms of satisfaction.

Once we conclude, based upon all of our experiences, that we are ready to find a way to peace, we let go of the biases that have barricaded our heart.

- We unravel the threads of discontent that have strangled us; and we assume the repose of our inner being, which is our true Self.

- We assume the daring adventuresome soul that we are as a whole Self; and we reach out of our safe hiding place from behind our carefully cultured face.

- We stretch out of our misapprehensions, break through the crusts of our apathy, shatter the void of our emptiness, and fill with radiance!

In allowing our spirit to be our real and present Self in the *now* world where we live every day, we release all that we have been.

- Our senses awaken, expand and increase; and we are filled with enthusiasm and a zest for all of life.

- We realize that our personal presence is divine.

- Our concepts stretch.

- Our vision becomes crystal clear, and trust is born.

- We trust all that we perceive and all that before was unfathomable to us.

- We trust in ourselves to discern and to act with wisdom.

- We trust that we can resolve any situation that arises.

These are the impact of living from our heart, the impact of living openly and sincerely, the impact of being open to the at-one-ment of the angels who are with us.

Hearing the angels is easy once we learn to trust ourselves. Hearing their guidance enhances our ability to trust ourselves. In fact, hearing the angels is the single-most powerful agent to living aligned with divine will ... and is our foremost experience of being human.

4

How to See the Angels

As Our Compassion Grows

Believing in the angels comes in that eternal part of us that breathes the divine fire: our spirit.

Once we realize our conscious link with Spirit, we are able to envision the presence of the angels. Once we are open to receiving the wisdom of our Higher Self—through our mind—we are able to begin noticing the fine etheric outlines of the angels around us. Once we are enjoined in the simplicity of goodness—borne within our heart—we are willing to be guided by those eternal beings of light who are our counselors.

Angels bring to us their whole Selves. They hold nothing back from us. They totally immerse us in their light. They fully blend their energy fields through us, and relay their ideas into our mind so we may imagine their concepts in words. The angels devote themselves to us with all of their glorious presence.

Once we awaken to our inner presence, which is always communicating to us, we begin to see the energy presences of these beings of light, whom humanity calls the glorious representatives of the Divine's love, will, and intelligence.

The Source of Insight

The angels are our benefactors during all of our days on Earth, and they are the reasoning of our innermost wisdom. It is their influence guiding us that gives us concrete insight and direction during our real-life circumstances. It is their attitude that we are able to live as our higher life *presence* that motivates us to live more in goodwill toward others. It is the angels' surrounding of our consciousness with hope and joy that is the Divine impressing us with truth's texture and real and substantial energy.

Once we alter our illusions from vague notions and crippled thought processes toward clearly understanding what is true for us—in any situation—we are being overtly influenced by the wise counsel of our angels. They are saturating us with their deep wisdom and seeding us with their divine insights, so that we may become attuned to our own glorious Self.

Those Four Angels Nearest to Us Are Our Ancestors

The angels who stand with us, day by day and night by night, are the ancestors of our own eternal Self. They are friends who have been with us since we first became conscious as a soul. They are the brothers of our whole Nature, the sisters of our original Person.

These angels are with us at all times. Their function is to arrange our energy field so that we gradually become so aware of the frequencies of life that we tap into the essential quality of the Universal Mind—by releasing all that we know and just *being* in the energy embrace of the "cosmic oneness."

Angels are not physical beings, although they may surprise us at times by appearing as a man or a woman. They do not need bodies; they are more evolved than the third dimension. However, because they are the agents of our personal growth and the caretakers of our spirit, they do sometimes present themselves when we are in a very great need.

The angels who work personally with us define our process of unfolding into higher consciousness. They give us the tools and techniques by which to enhance our mental capacity and emotional healing. They reveal to us—generally through dreams and meditations—our spiritual makeup. They teach us about our human perceptions and about our soul.

The few very dear angels, with whom we personally have walked for the several millennia of our spiritual existence, visit us regularly—both in our mind's eye and in the physical world. They stand before us in the full splendor and radiance of holy entities who carry the insignia of the Divine.

In the Rapture of the Angels

When we are instilled with the inner vision of an angel's presence, we feel the shower of its vibration trickling through us. We feel a wave of serendipity enthrall us and warmth caress our heart. We surrender to all of the lovely senses of our wholeness, and we are enraptured.

The angels, one or more, show themselves to us when we need to be aware of their substantial existence and when we are in need of them, whether because of danger or emotional distress.

We can learn to attune to the angels' energy presence more

directly. We do this by freeing our personal ego of the need for attachments and healing our ego of judgments, condemnations, and restrictive attitudes.

Then we begin the arduous task of self-enhancement, which is developed by our regular continuous adherence to the synergy of our soul's consciousness.

As we, through any number of practices, such as meditation, learn to acquire this mental link with our soul, we simultaneously are acquiring a link with all higher beings, including ascended masters and angels. As we develop a bond with the inner knowing of our soul, so we simultaneously are enhancing our connection to the angels who stand with us.

In this process of raising our energy frequency to higher and higher pitches and tones, while in the embrace of our awakening mind, we are leaving behind all of those arrogant characteristics that have bound us to unhappiness. We are releasing all of the angry feelings that have bound us to our inept and sorrowful past self. We are relinquishing all of the despondent and burdensome beliefs that have thwarted our innate delight for being.

Eventually this process becomes more easy and pleasant than trying and challenging. At that point, we are on the threshold of connecting with the angels who live beside us. It is then that we actually at times feel their presence, at times consciously hear their thoughts to us, at times see (in our inner eye) their delightful auras about us. These are the natural effects of releasing our ideas about being inadequate.

In the Embrace of An Angel

Being in the hold of an angel is a lot like being in our mother's embrace when we were first born. The sense of devotion between us and the angel is palpable. The angel's sense of desire for our well-being is a strength upon which we draw. The angel's affection for us and all that we are is a hope to which we cling. The freshness and peace we feel is our at-one-ment with that angel.

In this way, we begin to consciously know the presence of the Divine in our life. In this way, we are overlighted by all that we have sought to believe. We engage the sweetness that is inherent in our nature. We cultivate the devotion to all that is inherent in our character. We invest our attention to becoming as content as we can.

These are the effects of the angels upon our human vibration. They surround us with their love. Once we feel their love flowing through us, we have begun the phase of *seeing* the angels. It is in the inner vision of our heart that we open to the presence of these etheric beings. Their light is luminous and clear and radiates about them with the full spectrum of a rainbow.

On the Wings of An Angel

Imagine this:

In a shower of lights and reflections, amidst an extravagant display of the power of the Divine, stands an illuminated Being smiling at you.

This Being is so grand that you fall in awe before its beauty. It reaches over to touch you with its radiance, and you feel a rush of light whoosh through you from your crown to the soles of your feet.

You feel your whole being expand, your heart swell, and your breath open. You see the eyes of the angel through the brilliant light around it. Its eyes are deep and endless and crystal clear.

As if you are thinking it, the angel spreads its light around you and you see yourself in the midst of that cold etheric fire.

The fire is the eternal life awakening in you, brought *into* you by the angel who gives you that very important ability to see it.

The angel then expands its presence, as if raising wings of light, and you ascend with the angel into a timeless realm.

Within the cloak of the angel's wings, you flow through the ages behind you. You see the lives of humanity as if before you on a screen. You feel the hurts and pains of humanity as if thorns in your own spirit. You feel the hopes of humanity as if borne in your own soul.

The angel carries you in its wings of light throughout existence. You see worlds that are evolving much like our own Earth. You see peoples of other dimensions, and beings of all the realms.

In the light of the angel's wings around you, you feel safe, and you know that all of life is but an extension of your own, that you are an extension of the fire of God who breathed you.

Then you come back into the awareness of your form. The light that is brilliant and all around you gradually withdraws. The angel's eyes diminish gradually from your sight, which is the clearest memory you keep with you.

Afterwards, whenever you feel the breath of the angel's song upon you, this memory awakens. The angel's eyes appear in your mind. You remember the angel's smile. You remember the angel's wings of light around you. You know that you are a part of its great presence.

You begin to feel the senses of the angel through you. You feel a bond building between you and the angel. You feel your reasoning mind absorbing the eternal knowledge of *All That Is.*

At this point, you are about to reawaken your own great Self's full presence. You are on the verge of unmasking your own delightful aura and letting it glow more clearly than ever before. You are beginning to understand the power that resides in you.

Angels stimulate in us what we already know. They guide us not only with our daily struggles; but they remind us of what we already are, and lead us to the inner place where we may recognize our own glorious soul.

5

Origin of the Angels and Humanity

The Face and Form of God

Since the beginning of existence of all life, at the earliest moment of beings, angels have been in the service of the Divine. They are the unique representatives of the Consciousness. They are the voice of God and the face of God, and they perform the tasks that we humans attribute as functions of God. God is an energy. God is mind. Angels are the *form* of that energy.

We are in the blessed presence of these entities. They are at all times available to us through our heart. They are the inner reasoning that speaks to us. They are our emotions when we are aligned. They are our thoughts when we are clear.

After angels came to be, as a result of the Consciousness expanding Itself, they were full of the potential to express the Divine Mind. At first, they lived only to serve the light of all life. But after humanity—and other life forms—evolved from the Divine's expansion, the angels became humanity's helpers.

The angels do not pretend to be *our* mental creations. Neither do they tell us of their true existence ... until we need to know, which varies with each of us. At first, we understand only that our needs are being met in unusual ways.

It is the angels' responsibility—elected by them—to tell us when we are being overly enthralled with our own little escapades. They give us promptings to lead us forward in our life's journey toward deeper insights as to the meaning of life.

They enhance our ability to perceive and comprehend the mystical explanations of what life is about. They help us gradually learn to imagine the world as a place of mystery ... by raising our curiosity so that we long to explore the aspects of being human that we have least understood.

How Connecting to the Angels Makes Life Easier

We attune to the unseen and inexplicable forces through the energetic influence of the angels. They instill us with a capacity to reason through our unconscious mind—that part of the Universal Mind from which our conscious mind draws perceptions about the nature of reality.

The angels swiftly put into our heart and imagination the ability to delve into our deeper Self and the psyche of our unique original being. They reach into the desires of our supreme Self and help us to stretch our ability to perceive the unfathomable aspects of nature, those events and circumstances that to us seem to contradict the known.

Once we are open to any possible reason for a strange occurrence, we are open to angels appearing to us in the process of leading us to safety. We are also open to angels giving us very particular information about our own life so that we better understand the underlying relationships that build our character. The angels also give us information about our future.

In attending to the details of the underlying causes of our suffering, we receive "intuitive flashes" from the angels. This is a primary way they enlarge our understanding about situations and how they impact the directions in which we are emotionally traveling.

With intuitions, we learn to be more "at-one" with the events of our life; which seem, at times, to guide us in directions we least wish to go. However, when we do listen to the *knowing* part of us that pushes, urges, and sometimes speaks with insistence, we learn that our obvious choices are not necessarily the choices that will give us true joy.

We discover, as we mature—more from our years of experience than by chronology—that our clearest moments in life are found not in our great ideas nor our enormous efforts. Rather, the moments of our intimate self-truths are those few most powerful experiences that release us from the abundance of our misconstrued ambitions. It is these single flares of clear thinking that give our life purpose. It is this inner repose of our clear instincts that is the anchor to which we hold as we strive to shape our life.

Such events are the angels utilizing their inner links with us to show us their all-powerful grasp of the more relevant points of view that will help us to attain joy and peace in our whole being. Through our instincts, intuitions, and knowing to explore a particular avenue of thought, we awaken to the wisdom of those beings whose sole purpose is to serve us.

The angels are not duty-bound, but they reap their highest satisfaction by teaching us how to hear our loving Self. They give us aid because we are akin to them in our true Self. They support us once we know the value of the light of cosmic consciousness.

When Humanity First Existed

Angels lift our despair and guide us into hope because once—long before we became human—we were a part of that vast entourage of angels who came into being from The Unmanifest, which is called "The Before Time."

When humanity first existed, we still appreciated the farthest reaches of that power. We were without human bodies and free of emotions. As we became human, in flesh and with all the delusions of this limited insight, we lost touch with the Realms of our brothers and sisters who did not come with us.

Those who remained attuned to the perfection of The One Great Heart are now the advisers who guide us through the underlying themes that direct our lives and evolve the soul consciousness in us. Those angels who remained centered in the truth of the Bliss are the inner counselors who now tenderly and accurately influence our objectives, plans, and desires.

Those angels who remained in joy live in eternal recognition of the order of things. They see the patterns that rule life. They realize the details that shape physical reality. They perceive the links between our thoughts and the forms in energy that then manifest.

The angels' view of our world is broader than our own because their presence is not confused. Their minds are not caught in illusions of power or fear. They reason through senses that control a vision of the whole.

The angels devise the strategies that help us to build toward inner peace. They lead us into recognizing our own potential as creative beings. They instill in us the motivation to express our soul, that eternal part of us that is free of human conditioning.

When You Need an Answer

My friends, whenever you need an answer, trust that your *instincts* are your angels showing you the way.

Whenever you are distraught, live in the arms of the angels' comforting embrace; which you can feel envelop you, bathing you in a sweet repose.

To escape your pain, allow the inner healing of forgiveness to flow through you, which opens your heart to your soul.

Whenever you are dismayed or afraid, call upon the angels to instill in you an insight of right action.

> Then be *still.* Go into the silence of the realm of your inner being. Reside there until you begin to let go of your mental dissertations.

> Sound the *OM*, the universal tone of at-one-ment. Sound the *OM* from the center of your being. Sound the *OM* with all of your feeling. Sound the *OM* clearly and softly.

> Feel the tone of the *OM* resonating through you. Continue sounding the *OM* until you feel your rigidity beginning to dissolve and your barriers fall.

Then open your heart. If you feel the need to cry, let yourself cry. If you feel the desire to laugh, let yourself laugh. Let tears and laughter heal you. Let tears and laughter release you from the safe controls you have built within you.

Then emerge out of the silence. Open your eyes and, with an open heart, feel the world around you. Trust the intuitions that fill you, flood you. Allow the images that flash into your mind. Be still and look at them. Study and feel the impact of those images.

Trust the intuitions you feel about the images. Accept the import of what you are aware. Do not censor your intuitions, do not stop them. Let them flow, study them. Learn to understand how they *are* your higher vision guiding you.

Now let go. Come back into your fully awake self. Bring with you the warm sense of that *Presence* guiding you.

6

The Mind and Embodiment of God

Through Angels We Access the God Mind

We are able to understand our personality by the presence of the angels who work with us. Angels open our mind and release our inner confusion. They are the speaking presences of our higher Self. They invoke our personality's highest abilities, such as attunement with our godself.

In the bountiful embrace of the angels, we are receptive to the Universal Mind. Angels open our consciousness to other levels of reality. They are, in fact, the *inner voice* that speaks to us when we are distraught. It is the angels who say to us, *Be still.*

Angels realign our goodness and prepare us for the finer frequencies of our being. In the embrace of angels, we are uplifted, renovated, and developed. Angels play such an important part in our growth that it is almost impossible to receive the spiritual presence of the Divine Mind without the angels' accompaniment. Angels actually function as intermediaries. In fact, they represent the Divine to us. It is the angels we hear when we are receiving the thoughts of the Universal Powers.

The Voice of God

So, how is it that the angels play such an important role in our lives and we are so vaguely aware of them? How is it that they do not appear before us more frequently, or that we are not open more consciously to receiving their advice? We do not realize that we can.

In the divine realms of our multidimensional being, we *do* understand the laws of life and realize the angels' presence. However, as a human, we are *un*consciously involved with our Higher Self most of our life. In fact, our Higher Self presence is an anomaly to us for many lifetimes. It is only once we reach the level of self-awareness that we are much more than a physical self that we can even fathom that angels are real, and then it is only a worship from afar. Even then, we do not truly see them as the necessary agents of our lives; we do not acknowledge that they are the very real agents of the Divine, which directs our intuitions.

It is the angels who reassess us when we are "connected" to our center. It is the angels who offer us their wisdom into our consciousness. It is the angels who help us to comprehend that we are able to live in a state of mind that is free of judgment and free of fear. The angels are our friends as well as our teachers. They counsel us, but also inform us.

They Await Our Heart's Invitation

We learn to contact the angels by reassessing ourselves. When new in our search of Self, we open our mind to studying and evaluating our personality. When we begin to analyze who we are and how we have evolved, we are taking the first step toward being available to the angels' direct influence.

Angels are always present, but they cannot as fully influence us without our effort toward self-awareness. So, the most significant level of being able to *hear* the angels is made possible by opening our heart and mind to our personality's issues.

We learn to heal our body, heal our psyche, and heal our mind. During this process, we gradually become aware that angels live beside us, that they are always at our side and as near to us as our own breath.

This process is the most empathetic access we have for *feeling* the presence of the angels. The rush we feel, the chills up the spine, the intuitive inner link; these are the *inner voice* speaking to us or, more exactly, our angel guardians guiding us.

However Long It Takes Us, They Are Here

It may seem odd to think that angels link with us so intimately. Why do they? And how can we believe it is really so?

I had been a student of the spiritual life for twenty-five years when I became aware that angels are at my side in everything I do. Actually, this realization came as a surprise, because I hadn't imagined that angels are so very present in so many ways. In fact, if I had realized this before, I might have felt threatened or somehow powerless. To think that angels are so closely involved with me would have frightened me, because I would have felt I wasn't in control of my own life.

However, now I have learned to appreciate the idea ... because I have learned my limitations. I have learned to open my whole being, and now I am very aware that I do nothing alone, that angels are always present and at my side.

Angels are not invisible. They also are not human or physical. They are light. While I am seldom able to see them as personages, I frequently have *seen* them and not realized it. Angels are the movement that flashes by the corner of my eye, the "fog" that sometimes drifts before my vision, the lights that flicker in my head. They also are the illumination I sense around others.

It is now fathomable to me that angels are my own inner thoughts and that they speak to me at all times. Since I am now more available to the divine energy, I hear them nearly unceasingly and I know now that is the angels. Wow.

It is truly interesting to me that I am only now beginning to *see* the angels. I almost can barely contain my joy. At last!

Well, I am sure that as I continue to grow in self-empowerment, I will become even more conscious of these very powerful friends, because I am just beginning to truly sense them. It is, therefore, my earnest wish to share this self-discovery, because I feel the incredible impact this knowledge can have upon all of humanity.

Consciously communicating with the angels is, I feel, the most important step we can make toward integrating with our own divine Self; because, more than any other single element, learning to hear and respond to the angels' guidance enhances our lives.

Besides, that is the angels' function. That *is* what they do. That is why they exist. That *is* their purpose of being.

7

The Four Angels Who Help You Every Day

The beliefs that we humans carry often embroil us in confusion and fear. We often forget who we are able to be, because we are absorbed with daily life and our relationships. We feel it is more important to get through the day than attend to our spiritual yearnings for a peaceful mind and calm heart.

How, then, is it possible that the angels can help us with our human struggles? I cannot begin to thoroughly describe the angels' functions; however, I will try.

As given from the Angels of Serendipity, there are four categories of angels who personally work with each of us on a continual basis. First, we look at the most commonly identified category, the guardian angel.

Guardian Angel

Our personal *guardian angel* surpasses all of our imagination's concepts of what guardian angels do. They have a lot more to do than just save us from danger.

- Our guardian angel illuminates our path with its splendid *insights.*

- Our guardian angel illuminates our inner consciousness with *perceptions* of what will help us personally resolve our various tasks and options.

- Our guardian angel frees our perceptions about reality and delineates *what is possible* for us.

Each of us is unique and has an individual purpose. Each of us is in life to learn something special for our soul awareness. Our guardian angel helps us to imagine what we are able to be, stretches our perceptions about what we are able to conceptualize, instructs us in comprehending the various attitudes that block our visions of life, invokes our compassion for others, and, at times, even rescues us—if that will prevent us from making an error that would be more deterring than we could personally endure.

Our guardian angel, therefore, has many functions other than saving us when we are in trouble. In those instances, this angel is allowed—by universal truth—to intervene only if we are not yet able to help ourselves, and if we still have not completed our purpose for this lifetime. Our guardian angel does not intervene if we no longer are required for service toward others at this particular juncture of our eternal being.

Whether or not we are assisted during a dire circumstance varies from individual to individual. Each of us does have protection, but we must consciously invoke it. Our personal guardian angel can intervene only if we recognize the necessity of outside assistance when facing a threat to our existence in the body.

So, in imagining a guardian angel working with you, envision a being whose purpose far exceeds one that rescues you from various difficulties. Rather, envision a being who assists you in various capacities to fulfill your life's commission for being an enlightened person and, ultimately, a teacher to others.

Each of us has a definite task to perform while on Earth. We each have a purpose. Our individual insights guide us to that particular desire and intention; until we become attuned spiritually, mentally, emotionally, and physically.

Whether or not we can see the impact we may be having upon others, nevertheless we are all teachers. Whatever our personal growth may be, each of us is teaching at least one other person what is possible in life.

This is also the primary function of our guardian angel; to enhance our awareness, so that we consciously participate in the unfolding of our higher Nature.

Following is the viewpoint of those angels who serve as humanity's personal guardians.

Living in the light of God, these beings vibrate as perfect expressions of *The Presence.*

We become attuned to our personal guardian angel when we open our vision to the realities of the inner kingdom; because guardian angels are intangible and, although extremely intelligent, they vibrate at a frequency of the life force far beyond what we, as incarnates, know.

As incarnates, it is our delightful opportunity to bridge the etheric distance between our own earthly world and the celestial kingdoms. This is not impossible and actually is quite common among humans; because the angels are quite fond of us and do everything they can to assist us, so that our lives will be smoother and more sweet in the kinder aspects.

- Our guardian angel listens to our prayers, contains our dreams, and uplifts our demeanor into our highest aspect.

- Our guardian angel lifts our vision into the divine Being we call God.

- Our guardian angel alleviates our dismay, protects us from despair, and controls outer forces that would destroy us without our permission at the soul level of our consciousness.

- Our guardian angel offers us its incredible perspective about life ... until we become so at-one with our natural divine Character that we live that Character while in the physical body.

- Our guardian angel helps us to reach the levels of attunement wherein we can receive the higher vibrational energy presence of our master teacher, who is an evolved ascended Being who once was human and gained an enlightened vision of existence.

- Our guardian angel, therefore, serves as an intermediary in much the same way as a friend who comprehends the greater Self we are and listens to our yearning to be more useful.

This describes the overall tendency of guardian angels, yet these angels' service goes much deeper.

Imagine this:

It is dawn and you have wakened from a very deep restful sleep. There are no sounds. The night is silent. You are wide awake and you do not understand why you have suddenly opened your eyes out of a dream and become aware of the world around you. You wonder what wakened you.

Then a voice speaks into your heart, *Good morning. I am here.*

Counselor Angel

When we divulge to others our dismay, our personal *counselor angel* intercedes for us by sending us contemplative thoughts and visions of our true Character, which is powerful and joyful.

- Our counselor angel invests us with a perception of all that we are.

- Our counselor angel intercedes frequently during our day-to-day existence.

- This angel illuminates our process of self-discovery and

leavens our emotions (as much as possible) by continuous reinforcement, encouragement, and direct contact, as required for our continued pursuit of self-awareness.

- Our counselor angel is responsible for our becoming at least somewhat more sensitive to our true Nature, to who we essentially are.

- Our counselor angel continuously presents to us alternatives of possibilities for the various avenues available to us.

When we cannot perceive a way out of a situation, our counselor angel gives us direct insights into our consciousness and a splendid comprehension of the full spectrum of our existence, character, and abilities.

- Our counselor angel functions as a demonstration of our unique promises.

- This angel, no matter who we are or what we do, continuously instills us with the possibility of being more than we have believed ourselves to be.

- Our counselor angel recognizes our inner light and is always functioning as a voice of hope, inspiration, and motivation.

It is our counselor angel who causes us to exceed our perceptions of what is possible and teaches us to evolve into the most extraordinary human being we can be; which is always within us, waiting only to be invoked, accepted, and applied.

Caretaker Angel

Our personal *caretaker angel* specifically delights in holding a focus of our strength, to which we then align.

This angel concentrates its vibration into our body, emotions, and mind, with a continuous presence of divine values and attitudes.

- Our caretaker angel teaches us self-will.

- Our caretaker angel illuminates those qualities within us of our resistance to the light, and enhances our abilities in the spiritual strategies for living in honor.

Without our caretaker angel's presence, we are void of the higher wisdom that infuses our everyday perceptions for living in right action.

- Our caretaker angel is, in fact, chiefly responsible for giving us a broader perspective of truth.

- This angel caretakes our spiritual identity by illuminating the values of our eternal solidarity with our Cosmic Self.

With our caretaker angel's impact in our physical life, we are more inclined to contemplate our place in the universe, because our caretaker angel gives us the yearning to discover what else there is in life besides struggle.

Intercessor Angel

Our personal *intercessor angel* bridges the "void" in our being and links us with those divine Persons who exist in life as nonphysical *consciousnesses* who have evolved beyond physical reality and are humanity's ancestors and predecessors; they are currently living, but their bodies and dimensions are unlike our own, because their energy frequency is light rather than density.

Our personal intercessor angel connects us with our Higher Self, but also with those illuminated conscious beings who exist independently of humanity, those enlightened souls who were once human.

Over history, those beings have been called ascended masters. They actually exist in *our* world but within a much finer dimension than most of us are consciously able to see, feel, or touch. People who are clairvoyant and see beyond the third dimension actually see these beings' forms, which are luminous and nonsolid.

Parable: The Subtle Difference Between Dimensions

Envision this:

> See yourself at a table with a friend. You are both about to share an apple.
>
> Imagine that you cut the apple into three parts.
>
> Imagine that you take one part of the apple yourself, which is essentially solid. Give your friend another portion of the apple.

Now envision your friend, who is holding a portion of the apple, beginning to vibrate into a less solid image yet is still visible to you. A good analogy is "wavering as heat off a pavement in July"—visible.

You and your friend both eat your portions of the apple. Your portion feels crunchy and juicy to taste. As you swallow, it feels quite solid.

You watch your friend eating the other portion of the apple in the same way. To your friend, that portion of the apple is just as solid and juicy as your own was to you ... yet you can see that your friend is not as solid as you and is a wavering image before you.

Now take the third portion of the apple and set it at the table before the empty chair. Imagine that sitting in that chair is a being of a much finer vibration than your friend. You do not physically see that being, but you *feel* something there; you have an awareness or sensation of a *presence*.

The back of your neck tingles or you may have another sensation that indicates something different in that third chair other than empty space. You intuit that perhaps an angel or your master teacher is present, so you offer the third piece of apple as a gesture to contact and bridge the realms, the dimensions.

Imagine as if that being *is* there and takes the third piece of the apple. In your outer vision, the apple suddenly disappears. In your outer vision, the apple no longer exists. You see nothing before you, but you *feel* the sensation of *something* present that you cannot see or identify through your usual senses.

If you were to see this being, he or she essentially would look like any of us. He or she would look real. He or she would enjoy the third piece of apple with the same flavor, crunchiness, and juiciness that you did yours. However, to your perception (in the denser reality) that person and the third piece of apple are not visible.

This is a very crude description of the frequency differences among beings who exist at different energy levels.

How to Connect to the Higher Dimensions

Well, our personal intercessor angel carries an energy or vibration of such measure that it bonds us with the other dimensional realities. This angel's presence synchronizes our human energy pattern and vibration, at whatever degree we personally might be vibrating, from the most dense and most solid human to the highest vibration possible as a human yet still functioning in a physical body.

As we humans ascend in self-awareness and the various qualities that attend that awareness, our vibration increases and our body's density lightens. Scientists have acknowledged that the human body is not solid but is largely space. We are energy in motion.

As we become more attuned to our divine Character and more illumined by inner serenity and compassion and all of the qualities that attend that, the vibration of our being (largely space and energy in motion) vibrates at a quicker pace and increases the space of our being between the atoms and molecules; so that, although visually we still look solid, truthfully we are more spacious than before.

There is more space between the parts of our being, and the energy movement of our atoms and molecules is more rapid and increasingly so in all of these factors as we become more and more attuned to the energies of the life force. So, we become more light.

How All Dimensions Co-Exist At Merely Different Vibrational Frequencies

Likewise, those beings whom for centuries humanity has given the titles of master, guru, Christ, ascended one—all who at one time were human or physical—are in such a fine body of light that to us they seem invisible ... yet they are just as real as us. They are just as real as the apple pieces in the various degrees of lightness or density, yet still existing and still tangible within that particular focus and dimension.

Dimensions are not compartments that are clearly delineated. Dimensions are a *continuous* evolution of energy or vibration that *gradually* becomes more spacious and moves faster. That is the only difference between dimensions.

So, more literally, rather than being separate as third, fourth, fifth, etc., dimensions are continuous in much the same way as water is continuous yet manifests in various forms, depending upon the level of its energy pattern, from water to steam to gas to vapor to invisible.

So, when we are assisted by our personal intercessor angel in making contact with those beings who exist in *our* world, even in *our* dimension but in its finer *resonance;* we are also infused with the knowledge of the existence of those beings who guide, instruct, and imbue us with the properties and wisdoms of the universal whole, whom humanity generally identifies as God, or the Divine.

Those beings who accept their identity as all love and who exist solely in the vibration of all love invest us with their capacity for love so that *we* too may rise in our own experience of what love is and how to be loving.

The Energy Bridge Between Us and Ascended Beings

Our personal intercessor angel provides the energy bridge between those higher beings' vibrations and energies and our own. Our intercessor angel links us with those beings so we can more distinctly feel and be aware of the finer frequencies that are at all times around us and a part of our existence, although unseen.

In this sense, the universe is one. The universe is a continuous *phasing* from the most dense to the most light, without compartments or distinctions from one level to another. The universe is a *continuous* evolution of the *energy* becoming lighter and lighter.

The primary characteristic that distinguishes our personal degree of lightness is how, effectively, we embrace and actualize the vibration we identify as love. Love *is* an energy. It is an energy we *feel.* Even love as we accept the term in our lives has many different degrees of lightness, from the most dense to the most pure. Yet love is energy.

Our goal, therefore, as a being is to access that love energy. Our process throughout our many lifetimes is to so imbue our self with the love energy that love becomes our entire focus for existence.

The *process* is how we uplevel that energy from its most dense to a lighter and lighter resonance in the quality of being we are.

So that, we are continuously striving to exhibit the qualities that we attribute to being loving—until such point that we *are* that energy and love exudes from us.

How *We* Ascend Into Our Higher Being

Our goal, therefore, toward attaining self-awareness is to *be* the love vibration at its most light frequency. Once we attain the finest frequency of love possible for maintaining a physical structure, we transcend the cycle of physical reality and move on to an even more fine degree of the light.

That is what the ascended beings have accomplished. They are so filled with the divine vibration that they have transcended the more dense levels of love and awareness and have ascended into a finer frequency of the Divine Presence.

They now instruct us in order to show us the way to follow them. Our personal intercessor angel provides the energy bridge between our own being and the ascended beings, so that we may feel in us the presence of the Divine.

This essentially is the overview of the primary functions of the four categories of the angels (*guardian, counselor, caretaker, intercessor*) who work with each of us in our daily lives. These four angels are very much involved with us and, while we may not always be aware of them, even seldom or not at all, nevertheless they are always present.

What Is This All About?

It is about us *being* energy. We are vibrational beings.

All of life is this energy, merely in different shapes because of various compositions.

Angels also are energy, although at a different frequency than humans. In fact, the angels operate at a level of life that is just as real in their eyes as ours is to us.

All of life has similar characteristics, but exists in finer and finer frequencies of devotion to the Divine—which is *felt* as love.

8

When You Can No Longer Ignore the Small Inner Nudgings

The Misinformation Out There

Often, humans believe that only evil spirits may contact our mind. We resist the notion of *good* spirits as possible influences and presences in our lives. We deny that angels are beneficial, because we have been taught that no one is permitted to describe such powerful figures without dying from their curses.

There is much misinformation about these beings who surround us in the realms of Spirit. So, many people are afraid if they have *any* experiences that seem supernatural. Our imagination has caused us to be misled about the angels' roles in our lives. For these reasons, most of the time the angels do not contact us concretely; so when we do encounter them, we cannot see them, we are afraid and we do not believe in their support.

Even when we do realize the significance of influences from the spiritual realms, often we imagine that such control is negative rather than useful to understanding the unfolding patterns we exhibit in our own character. Our interactions with Spirit become much like a game of "who is on the mountain?" or "who can win the prize?" We feel that unless we are in control of our experiences—by effort and by manipulation of every choice—fundamentally, an undercurrent of evil must be trying to misdirect us.

Humanity's misunderstanding of angelic beings, as portrayed in some paintings, gives this idea credibility. However, let us envision the true character of the angels whose sole purpose is to inform us of opportunities and to instruct us with instinctual knowledge about apparently otherwise unknowable truths.

Let us explore an encounter with an angel of the service that directly influences our existence in the human body, remembering that life is an exemplary experience for reflecting into our heart what we need to observe and study so that we will make choices to improve our beliefs and habits of character.

Parable: Life's 2x4 (for those who ignore the inner nudgings)

On the first day that we become aware of an influential powerful presence outside of our own mind and will, our state of mind is something like this:

We delight in our own unique perspective about the world and our domain, which we feel is the ultimate testimony of our individuality and our presence as a person who impacts the third dimension reality. It is our precious, persuasive, and fond experiences that illuminate our prestige in the eyes of our peers. We feel extremely capable in all respects; because we are charged with a given task that we meet brilliantly, and we choose to outwit the persons who are competing for advantages in the realms of our exacting disciplines and expertise.

Once we have realized success and conquered our advantage point to the extreme of even denying power to any other who might have participated or contributed to our projected self-appraisal, we forget that others have helped us fulfill our particular goals, and we forget that we have only just realized that our power is extraordinary.

This is a reflection of our tenuous condition as an influential presence in our community, family, or job. We deny any self-awareness of being *in*capable, and we prefer not to dwell upon our feelings of unsureness. We live so completely in the illusion of our successes that we believe we have arrived.

Yet underneath our confidence resides our true Self's inner knowing and our *shakeable* self-acclaim that crumbles at a moment's weakness or affluential surprise.

When we do not recognize that the "powers that be" who have given us such majestic opportunity can just as easily take it away, because they also play by competitive rules, we are restricted to support the delusion of "who's on top?" We are also so persuaded by our desire to feel successful that any other option is unlikely but that we have acquired a position of supreme authority in our own little world's experiences.

Yet underneath it all, we are reluctant to acknowledge our misgivings, and we are unwilling to imagine how any personal advantage could have included another person's point of view or strategy.

So, when we are commanded by our misguided sense of proper tactics to secure our whim's desires, we are implicated in treachery; because we accept only the knowledge of current philosophical teachings, which tell us that only the strong survive, that only one who takes charge can succeed, that only when we are superior to our competitors can we be winners. This is the vision of the powerful position we seek so that we will never again be hungry or alone with our dismal and inflated ideas of who we are.

The characteristic reasons we give for taking an approach of denial, or explicitly demanding that others obey our wishes, is that we are much more astute than they; that we have an inner assessment of the total picture; that we are creatively and visually capable of extraordinary accomplishments in any realm we choose to attack with all the vicissitudes of the world's expectations of one who is a winner.

Yet underneath it all, we are trembling at our incapacity to be full-proof against what might become known to others. We know that we are filled with a sense of uncertainty; and we know we cannot keep up this facade forever, because we feel slipping away from us our very tenuous power. We know we have lived a lie and that the truer picture is not our expiation of financial wizardry but that we have acquired certain inroads into the tremendous and exacting command of human reason, which is "make a buck, make a buck, make a buck." We are so filled with this image of living in the highest fashion that we do not explain our behaviors to anyone who is not our equal, not even to those who appear to be more powerful than we.

Whatever our situation seems to be, we are not completely sure just how effective we can be. We are not completely certain just how long our success will last. We feel the breath of failure hot on the back of our neck. We feel the infuriating struggle to keep afloat, as if we are being pulled down by weights around our feet. We feel as if life is a thunderous waterfall in which we are striving to swim upstream and yet unable to reach the top. Overcoming us are all of the natural forces pushing against us every inch of the way.

Sounding Familiar?

My friends, how can any of us be so impressed with ourselves that we forget we are always in this struggle to ascend in our self-image of being exemplary in some way? Regardless of who we are, or what kind of domain we strive to be successful in, we each have our own divisive rules by which we have learned to survive in the realm of the socially acceptable and responsible behaviors.

So, when confusion begins to catch up with us and we feel ourselves being sucked under by whatever forces are sublimating our efforts, we thrash even more wildly, unable to grasp any means of holding onto our very uncertain and tenuous success. We feel as if the "powers that be" are always just ahead of us, unwilling to give us a hand up, unwilling to show us how to be as successful as they are.

We see our challenges as an upward battle that never ends and that we are striving all alone without any kind of support from anyone below us. We realize that every one of us is in the same struggle, and we affirm that *we **will*** survive—at all cost. So, we pull ourselves up, inch by inch and rise into that stream of seductive treason of our inner knowing Self. We cannot even contemplate any other way than "survive, survive, survive."

So When Do the Angels Step In?

Can we expect the angels to help us when we are being pulled under by the tides of life? Yes, we can. The angels are always available to us. We are never left alone. Never.

Once we give up our attitudes of "reach me through my unconsciousness" and "reach me at all cost in spite of what I say or do," we become able to hear the angels' insights to us—which come through our inner knowing Self's quiet voice to our waking mind.

Once we realize we are unable to achieve our goals on our own, we reach a point of acknowledgement that angels might be real after all. At least we hope so, because we are afraid we will not survive financially or emotionally unless someone helps us.

Escaping the Sinking Quagmire of "Out of Answers, Desperate" (but not ready to tell anybody)

This is the point in our experience when we begin to understand that the challenges we exacerbate are not as destructive as we perceive. They are, rather, opportunities to evaluate ourselves. This can present a lot of confusion. However, it is a confusion that results from opening our inner thoughts to a wider range of applying what esoterically is called "giving us enough rope." You understand.

Now, when we are tired of searching our inner Self's many and varied avenues toward the potential achievement of happiness, we have tried all of the avenues we can think of, and we are resolved that we cannot be successful without some kind of ingenious helper, we open our mind to the antiquated concept of spiritual intervention. We even plead with the Divine to help us, please. This is not exactly an attitude of promising consequence. Nevertheless, it does restructure our perspective and the way we perceive ourselves within society.

It is our adversities unscaled that releases our benign sufferings from controlling our existence. It is then that we are ready for some kind of angelic assistance and that we are accepted into the divine plan and process of being instructed about our true destiny—why we are really here.

Once we realize our inability to surpass the functionary requirements of future shock, and we are still unhappy, when insights *do* come into our inner consciousness we are able to understand. These insights were already present; however, before, we were not interested in listening to our profound and supportive brain work.

Now Real Help Arrives

All right, let us consider how an angel believes in us throughout all of our domestic and environmental struggles. Our personal angels observe our anguished and exaggerated emotional ravings. They contemplate our angers and our fears. They observe our inner processes that kindle the awakening of our searching for the outer support of the entity we call God, as we understand God to be.

Our personal angels realize the extent of our pain, which to us largely paralyzes and suffocates us. However, until we are ready and we ask for the angels' help, they are unable to provide real information directly into our conscious mind. It is necessary for us first to reach a point of releasing our demands and persuasive self-deceptions.

Once we acknowledge that we are strangling within our own

unclear perceptions, the angels are able to reach our consciousness via their supreme belief in our true Nature, which is *"to honor all as our equals."*

When we are no longer reaping the consequences of a narrow vision, we become able to understand what our mistakes have been in attitudes and behaviors. This does not mean we know *how* to change our responses and actions; however, at least we can understand them. This indicates our first inclination toward wanting to be advised by the supreme powers of the universe, whom we later come to perceive as angelic beings.

The forces we call angels are entities who exist in a dimension other than our own. They are frequently able to inspire us with their socially supportive concepts. Their entire demeanor indicates to us that happiness is not a product of effort or disgust with ourselves, but is acquired only by forgiving our past actions and attitudes toward the world.

Once we understand that the pain we have suffered is the result of accepting that no person is valuable, including ourselves, we are ready to heal our heart of our misguided viewpoints that have left us hungering for truth. We are certainly able, at this point, to exercise wisdom to a sufficient degree that we can completely reshape our personal reality and totally revamp the structure of our life. The result is an expressed position of:

> *"Help me, please. I have done all I can. I can do no more. I release myself to you. Please give me understanding and show me the way."*

This state of mind determines how easily we hear our inner consciousness bellowing to us through our dim awareness. In searching for truth, we discover that our personal consciousness is an aspect of the Divine. We begin to realize that the universal realities co-exist, at the same time, merely from varying points of reference.

Once we have reassessed the controlling patterns of others and our own personal life circumstances, we have *begun* the inner journey.

We do not determine this path by our intelligence, and we do not reason our way to it. It is a path of unleashing our heart's desires from the restraints we have placed there by our resistance throughout our life to our inner proddings.

How Do You Forgive Your Past and Start Over?

Let us reconstruct how it is possible to forgive all we have done before.

It is not only possible, it is this characteristic that distinguishes us from the multitudes of beings who have not yet acquired a sensitivity to their spirituality as an instrumental power for their physical survival and well-being.

Not only are we *able* to forgive our personal angers and destructive patterns, to whatever degree they have undermined our potential for being happy—we *must* forgive before we can envision our life in a way that reflects our true Self and true Character.

Once we do perceive our human self as unfolding in our personality as well as in the spiritual domains, we are able to perceive our vulnerability—not as a personal albatross but as an ingredient for healing our personality. This may result in forgiving others as well, but that takes a little longer. It is all a part of the process of healing the wounds of our mind and heart.

This constitutes how angels counsel us at all times and are always present in our inspirations and our visions toward an easier way.

Yet until we forgive our own misguided perceptions, we are not able to access the angels' counsel to us. That's why it is so important to stop and listen.

9

When Does Help Arrive?

Just Ask

When you are ready to be helped by the angels, ask for them.

This is an opportunity to release all you have imagined as primary in life and to begin reconstructing the behavior patterns that have strangled your vision of your personal worth.

Begin by listening to the *voice* that speaks to you softly *into* your mind and acknowledging that *inner counselor's* advice. Do whatever is possible and realistic in acting upon that advice. Plan your experiences and decisions based upon the insights that come *to* you.

In this way, you open your insight to your higher consciousness, which is sometimes angels and sometimes your soul speaking. Either way, the inner voice is a voice of compassion and alignment, with higher values.

The Inner Voice

The inner voice never asks any of us to harm our own body or any other's. The inner voice always encourages us to act with appreciation, sensitivity, and humility. We are not asked to display our intellect, nor to be arrogant in our demeanor. We are not requested or commanded to do anything we would find abhorrent or impossible for our character. These are delusions of the lower self.

Persons who are unstable emotionally *can* attract energies and presences of entities who are unevolved. You can know whether an unevolved being is trying to direct you, by the nature of the vibration you feel or the nature of the suggestion made. If an entity asks or demands that you behave in a certain way that would damage you or another, do not act upon that suggestion. Assume that you are not yet ready in your psyche to connect with the higher presence of your own divine Self. Know that more work needs to be done in clearing and balancing emotionally and in gaining a healthier perspective on goodness. Once you have reached the level of caring and compassion for all forms of life and all points of view, rekindle your link with the inner voice. Until that time, however, you are not ready to act upon the counsel that will come to you; because it is essential that you be able to discern the vibrations that influence your attitudes and behaviors.

Most important, in the experience of seeking and acting upon the inner counsel: always seek first to being aligned emotionally, intellectually, and psychologically.

As these aspects come into balance, we reach a place of harmony within and we feel harmony with others to a greater degree. Or at least we are able to allow ourselves and others to differ without feeling threatened, and we do not feel a need to correct others regarding how they live and choose to believe.

It is then that we are nearer ready for the level of listening to the inner counsel in a very specific way, more ready to accept and acknowledge the insights that come *to* us through the inner voice.

Is it Always a Voice or a Thought?

Sometimes the inner voice speaks quite clearly. Sometimes it is more subtle or abstract and, therefore, chooses other forms of communication besides thought. Sometimes you may merely have an impression—strongly felt—about a situation, person, or place. Sometimes the impression may be quite pronounced. At any time that you have a very strong resonance to a person, place, thing, or circumstance, it is wise to acknowledge your premonition or intuition about it; because, at a deeper level of consciousness, you are attuned to the vibration and you are resonating to the energy of that experience.

Our body and spirit respond and attune subliminally. There are different ways we acknowledge or recognize a situation that we do not yet consciously realize is positive or negative in its effect upon us.

How Can You Discern Between a Positive and Negative Choice?

A positive situation exudes in and through you expansively. You feel a sense of expansion, stimulated, positively excited, a sense of delight, a feeling of joyfulness. You feel as if you are glowing. You have a rush of energy, a rush of chills, or a tingling sensation through your body that is thrilling.

On the other hand, a negative experience may cause you to inwardly cringe or withdraw, to feel as if you want to immediately leave the situation and get out of it. You may feel yourself collapsing inwardly or collapsing energetically. You may want to hold yourself, hold your middle, cover your middle with your hands, or bend over. You may feel a kind of pain, physical or nonphysical. Somehow energetically—in whatever way it affects your emotions, body, spirit, or mind—you feel as if you cannot tolerate the situation and you want to leave or pull away.

In such a situation, no matter what intellectually you may think is proper behavior, it is very wise to immediately respond by dismissing yourself. Free yourself from that situation and leave immediately.

You don't have to know why. You don't have to understand the reason for it. You don't have to denounce or deny any other person present. Simply excuse yourself from the situation and depart immediately.

It doesn't matter if the other people understand your behavior. It doesn't matter what you think of them. It is not important that you explain your reason for leaving. All that matters is that for you personally this is not an appropriate place to be. It is not conducive to your health or well-being, so you depart.

Do not judge the others verbally nor in attitude; merely accept that is *their* reality. It works for them; it does not work for you. So, you let go and you take yourself out of the situation ... *immediately.*

The Inner Knowing

There are many ways the inner guidance directs our actions and choices. Primarily, energetically.

The *guidance* does not always come through our thoughts or a voice we think we hear. That is the least pronounced and least common form of angelic communication. Most frequently, we have impressions.

You may have a picture or an even a vague image flash through your mind, which may be subtle and very quick. Most frequently, you may simply have a sense of *knowing* that something doesn't feel right, or perhaps that something feels *very* right. That is the energy impacting itself upon your aura.

Energy is pronounced. We are all connected energetically. We are all linked through a web of energy. Each of us carries an energy field, an auric field, a vibration. We link with every other living and inanimate form in existence. We are tied to other energy forms energetically. Whether or not we can see it, we are all connected.

This is how, regardless of the location of where a person might be, we can energetically sense and know what that person is feeling, perhaps even thinking. This depends upon the level of our clarity and sensitivity to energy patterns or to a particular person, place, thing, or circumstance.

So, time and place are not limitations upon our sensitivity, because all in life is connected by energy.

Trusting the Inner Sense

All of life also exists simultaneously and nonlinearly. Although we experience events sequentially, we actually can bridge time—past and future—through our subliminal consciousness. We can tap into a situation and know whether or not we will be aligned with that situation. In this way, we can determine in advance whether to participate with an individual or a group of people or a function ... because we sense intuitively and energetically whether that would be positive and enhancing for us.

In this way, we can evaluate what circumstances will be harmonious and enhance our presence as a person becoming light; and what circumstances might destroy our light or dampen our spirit or perhaps even lead us in the wrong direction and astray. Every circumstance has the potential of affecting us in one way or the other.

As we become more attuned to the vibrations around us in life, we become more clearly aware of choosing persons, places, things, and situations that we feel intuitively (sense energetically) will uplift our spirit and help us to feel more connected, more joyful, and more abundant; as opposed to circumstances, persons, places, or things that would detract from our energy and cause us to feel less than we are, less than we can be, less than we want to be.

Expanded Self-Awareness

So, we learn to choose. We learn to consciously evaluate. We learn to consciously act upon what we sense and know ... then live it. This takes practice. More than practice, this takes self-honesty and self-reflection. In many ways, rather than being psychic perception, intuition is merely an extension of self-awareness.

We learn to know ourselves more astutely and to discern situations and circumstances more accurately. As we become more attuned in this way, we become more self-aware and more clear about what kinds of attitudes and behaviors align with us. We learn to choose more accurately where to be, when to be, and when not to be with certain individuals and groups. This discernment and evaluation process is learned. It comes gradually with experience. Largely, it has to do with being truthful about what feels aligned to us, or not, with who we are.

Although certain persons, places, and situations may affect us in a particular way, it is important to remember that circumstances and effects do vary. There are times when a person, place, thing, or situation will be positive and enhancing. There are times when it will not. Some situations are perfectly fine in and of themselves but not appropriate for the self. Some situations may be fine for most people, but sometimes appropriate for us and sometimes not.

Choosing Resonance

It becomes necessary, therefore, to be attuned at all times to the right place and right time, to be so attuned to our higher resonance, and our need as a whole Self evolving, that we know intuitively whether, on any given day (today, tomorrow, or next week), it is a right action to participate in a particular event.

This is not a matter of right or wrong. It is a matter of where we *need* to be. Will that situation at that particular time enhance who we are? Do we need the experience? Do we need to be with that person? Or is the circumstance neutral for us?

Sometimes a situation is neutral and it is our personal choice whether to participate. From my own experience, I have learned that, if a situation does not feel right, I do not participate. There are so many things I want to do, certain activities that require my attention, and certain people with whom I wish to be. Many events might be fine for others but are not appropriate for me; therefore, I do not participate. It all is a matter of choice and self-awareness.

Opening to Higher Possibilities

Can we be so open in our attitudes that life flows for us apparently without effort? Yes, we can.

The impressions that come into our consciousness are how the angels give us their wisdom. Our impressions are the angels' primary and distinctive form of caring for us.

Once we release our attitudes of conquering and belittling others, we become infused with a clarity of mind that resonates through us as if we are a crystalline tuning-fork. When we are capable of supreme pleasantness and fashioning a new course in our life (because we are overly tired of the way we have lived), we are ensuring our higher sensitivity by opening our ideas and visions to realms of thought that, before, frightened us.

It is important to alleviate the disillusionment that previously overcame us. It is even essential that we come to a self-awareness that invites a personal relationship with the angels ... until that relationship becomes our viewpoint about reality and our relationship with our fellow human beings.

When we experience relationships at the introspective level, we see others essentially as persons of extreme loveliness and very much as sensitive as we are, and we delight in extraordinary interactions with them. Such fine relationships come to our presence of mind because we realize that all people carry the universal truth within.

We even assume that all people, even animals, have been born with a perfect consciousness, waiting for an opportunity to expand their level of perception to a higher consciousness focus. We understand that all beings around us, even animals, are in life to enhance their consciousness to a higher degree than ever before in their spiritual evolution.

From this point of view, we contemplate our own place as a human on Earth. As we contemplate, we learn that we have a reason for being on Earth. Eventually, we understand that our every dream is a part of our higher awareness development, that our every ambition is a step in unfolding our higher consciousness.

Aligning to Higher Personality

It is desirable for us to dream and to desire improving our life. In fact, our eternal knowing Self is continuously stretching out of its old skin of beliefs and evolving in perceptions of what is right and divine.

Once we expand in our comprehension of life and the world, we are able to evaluate more deeply our personal relationship to concrete reality. We are even forced, in a way, to rethink our plans. At some point in our process, we are divorced, by the forces of life, from our previous demeanor that was a dilution of our true Self's character.

Our uncanny capacity to reshape our process and redefine our behaviors gives us the understanding that we are something more than a human being; that each of us is a being of light, expressing for a time in a body of desires and dreams, but able to experience the dimension of wisdom that increases as we clearly and demonstratively define the society in which we live. This can be an extraordinary experience!

It is essential, therefore, toward completing our pattern of self-exploration, that we realign with our higher Personality; which is, in a sense, our personal self but at a much higher vibration of understanding the universal laws.

Therefore, when we are ready to engage in the process of self-healing our past and all of those relationships that have burdened us (because of our grief over them), we most definitely are needing to unlock the sacred place in our innermost Self, which is the kingdom of God. God exists in the very center of life and is found through our inner Self's visions and beliefs in eternal compassion.

Kindling a New Level of Conscious Being

How do we learn to release our judgments about what is healthy and what is irresponsible? How do we convince ourselves of the validity of what we imagine as spirituality in its finest form?

We begin by understanding that all of us are awakening to the universal powers that lie dormant in our inner being. The universal powers blossom in us once we begin to grasp that being human is an opportunity to relinquish all aspects of self-denial from our eternal Character and Personality, which is always in us in some way.

This certainly can invoke a tremendous degree of confusion in the beginning of self-analyzing who and what we are. However, because we are being infused with a clarity of mind from our intention to understand, we are blessed with the capability to discern what circumstances will give us the necessary visualizations and wisdoms to interpret our life history in the total course of this particular lifetime (even though, when we wish to go deeper, we can extend that illuminating process of self-investigation into other lifetimes as well).

Let us suppose, for the purpose of being understood by the people who share our personal reality, that we demand from our higher knowing Self clear answers *now*. We demand to be given wisdom and to feel inspired. This is a common desire. We become so obsessive, initially, with uncovering our delusions and suppressed antipathies toward others, that we push, push, push for fast advancement.

Yet, my friends, we unfold as we will. Enlightenment cannot be rushed. We can only pursue it with a steady self-discipline. Reaching our inner light is much like peeling away the layers of an onion. We just keep at it until we finally have removed all of the delusions of who we truly are.

This formula for gaining self-knowledge is ancient. It was a technique practiced by the earliest humans on Earth. This technique is being rekindled now because: *Humanity, as a whole, is becoming conscious. As a whole, we are reaching a level of self-appreciation never before attained by the human species.*

Yet, while this is taking place (unconsciously for the many), those who know they are on this path can introspectively delineate exactly where they have been, why, and with whom. They can learn now of their mistaken ideologies and how to heal their misinterpretations. As they do, they become more confident in developing as a whole Self.

Learning to Live As a Higher Presence

How do we embrace this process when, essentially, it is not an overnight miracle?

We learn to be whole through continuously applying the universal laws, day in and day out. When we are open to receiving our inner voice's counsel, we are definitely in the process of becoming whole during our *current* lifetime. It is our ability to receive, acknowledge, and act upon the insights of our inner knowing Self that distinguishes one particular lifetime as the one in which we may ascend in the ability to know who we truly are, then be it.

We who walk upon this path can do so unashamedly. We can hold our heads high and walk as the angels do. This life is a blessing when we do. When we invest our higher presence as our vehicle for living, everything else that we do, think, and say comes from the center of our knowing Self. This can be an extraordinary experience. We can be so divinely inspired that nothing we have known before satisfies.

The belief that we humans are innately divine is ancient. *What we focus upon, what we give our attention to, is the manifest reality in which we live.* When we see our being as a lovely presence and we give ourselves over to living from our ideal Nature, we transcend the lower ideas, attitudes, and emotions that previously suffocated our spirit. When we relinquish our judgments of what is holy, we begin to truly walk in our light.

Devoted to the Bliss of Being Your Authentic Self

How do we embody the teachings of the ages without studying what the sages have written? How can we possibly accomplish in this present lifetime what it has taken several millennia for all of humanity to discover?

Individually, there are no limitations. *Socially, we are all reaching a turning point of consciousness as whole beings.* It is our willingness to walk in the light that makes it so.

When we are so devoted to bliss that nothing else is real, bliss becomes the world in which we live. Our devotion is the seed of our heavenly presence. When it begins to root in our personality and reach up into the light for nurturing, and we begin to open like a blossom—unfold, like a rose, one petal at a time—we are infused in every cell of our being with the divine light.

The angels are this light embodied. With their counsel and goodwill toward us, we more easily can access the light in us because the angels are the bridge to the light we are.

The angels are our mentors for how to be holy. We learn from their behaviors and ways of thinking and feeling that are free of distress and confusion. We learn from the angels how to believe in our own inherent beauty.

If the angels believe in us, surely we can also? If the angels trust that we are light, surely we can also? With all of their wisdom, for them to give us their time, surely we must be worth it? We are.

My friends, let not us not delay our journey. Let us walk in our light. It is who we truly are.

10

Your Talents Magnify

Increasing Serendipity

When we depend upon the angels for our concentration, we believe in their visions for our life. We learn that the angels indeed can give us their strength and support whenever we are able to accept it. We learn to envision our life free of limitation and to live unrestrained by our innermost fears. We even learn to encounter our deepest angers and to dissolve them without feeling regret or animosity.

It becomes quite important to us to rekindle the angels' voices as the guiding consciousness that enhances a smooth transfer from our being obnoxious and dependent, toward being kind, open-minded, and open-hearted in all circumstances. This attitude becomes relevant in all of our actions. We actually become dependent upon ourselves for energy, love, and freedom of mind.

There is in us a potential to step up in our vision's criteria of humility and serendipity: by envisioning ourselves as qualifying every choice by the sensory observations of our inner being. It is our inner visions that give us the strength to compare our behaviors between what we want to be and our inclinations that are sometimes over-reactive.

This self-evaluation becomes instrumental in our obedience to the universal truths. Once we reconstruct our character into a more supreme person of inner vision, we are less inclined to reach outward for control and direction. We are *inner* motivated and *inner* guided. This inner direction is a form of angelic guidance. Although we are able to function on the higher planes of consciousness without the angels' support, it is the angels' presence and divine vibration that uplifts our ability to be clearly attuned to our own higher reasoning personality, or higher knowing Self.

So, even though, in our own abilities, we are blessed with visions of self-empowerment, the angels may double, triple, even quadruple our strength by their belief in us and by their continuous presence that silently energizes our higher reasoning consciousness. The angels invest in us their capacity for an unlimited vision and a re-evaluation of every circumstance that we face.

In this perspective, let us imagine that you have been given a task that challenges your capabilities much more greatly than you have ever had to confront. Let us suppose that the visions you have had about being self-supporting are new to you and that you have not yet learned to accept this as tangible, even essential to your survival. It then becomes the very necessary task of the angels who watch and listen to your dramatic episodes to instill faith in you.

Anecdote: Financial Fears As a Self-Supporting, Temporary Secretary, Single Woman

Let me offer an example, a situation I myself overcame. I was a part-time employee in assorted job environments as a temporary secretary and word processor. This was fulfilling at first, although reluctantly endured by my inner nature. Nevertheless, rather than believe in my capacity to support myself energetically, financially, and emotionally with my own abilities to hear the counsel of the angels and my higher reasoning Self, I allowed myself to be dependent upon the path of less involvement, seeking a reliable necessary income.

This path was a lesser initiation. As much as I was denying my own abilities and God-given wisdoms, I had not yet realized that: *Many paths teach us our power.*

Working at jobs was, for a time, essential to my learning process of how to believe in my nature as a spiritual and worthy Self. I lacked confidence in my creative abilities and I struggled with self-esteem. So, for a time, I resisted the power of my own higher divine Self and "caved in" to the less strenuous way; which, in the long run, was actually much more difficult energetically.

Working at a job, of which I was capable but unhappy, reduced me emotionally to a confused and suppressed person. I lost touch with my inner power, forgot who I could be, and became a self living by *outer* regulations and time-frames rather than by listening to my inner counselor's advice and instincts.

During these years, I became continuously more absorbed in the drama and forgot my precious link with the angels. I forgot how incredibly powerful that link is, and I succumbed to my uncertainty about my previous inner knowing.

The Inner Angst

The day arrived when I no longer could tolerate the void I felt growing within me, as if I were falling apart inside. My whole vision of life was dissolving before me. My yearning to be giving and wise was fading away—because I was not giving myself what I needed and actually wanted.

That was the challenge, you see. I was afraid that my higher insight would not work, that my gift was too shallow and unusual to be considered helpful enough that I might be useful to anyone. I had lost faith in myself long ago.

Then came that day when I no longer could tolerate the struggle within me. I no longer could imbue my presence with doubt. I struggled, yes. I was unsure, yes. Yet I felt that if I did not alter my path, I would wither away and never attain happiness.

So, I accepted the challenge. I pulled myself up in my faith and turned to Spirit to re-nurture my connection. It was difficult at first to keep my spiritual flame alive, because I had lost it almost completely, I felt.

In the time after, however, when I committed my full attention to being aligned with my center and to reconnecting with my spiritual Self, I felt blessed by the presence of the angels all around me. They filled the rooms of my home and traveled with me everywhere I went. I could feel their hope imbuing my very being. I do not remember seeing them and, at the time, I did not know that my increasing conscious awareness was because of the angels' presence.

But, my friends, the angels stand with us, always. When we

are seeking a path of spiritual awakening or to strengthen our connection already born but forgotten, an innumerable team of angels supports us. They stand round about us and invest us with their consciousness—until we regain our strength spiritually and mentally.

I have learned that I can, indeed, be as clear as ever, and even more so. I have learned that by dedicating myself completely to the process of being spiritual, I can be everything I have imagined myself to be.

We learn to release our fears and not to let them direct our lives. We learn to understand the full *presence* of who we are and, over time, to believe in our inner counselor's advice.

It took me seven weeks of complete focus to reintegrate with my spiritual purpose, by giving my complete attention in every aspect of my days and nights, complete devotion, inner and outer, in every way.

I meditated every single day and, with each day, grew stronger. With each day, I gained greater clarity and inner knowing.

The *voice* that counseled me, as thoughts in my mind, had always been present, always connected; but now it became more and more strong as a *continuous* presence of encouragement and motivation. This *voice* continuously reminded me of what I needed to be doing, such as "Take your vitamins. Take your vitamins. Take your vitamins." I, therefore, found that the inner counsel is practical. It helps us to heal our body as well as our psyche. Whatever our needs, the inner voice can guide us into clearly and accurately responding to our highest potential.

After this period of seven weeks, in May 1994 I suddenly began to feel the *power.* It was extraordinary! It had been such a long time. I had missed the power. I felt *alive* again. *Real* again. I realized that without this connection to my spiritual identity, without this constancy of the *power* in me and through me, I was more of a living zombie than a real human being. It wasn't until I gave myself over to the yearning in my heart and spirit, and followed my inner reasoning, that I felt what I truly could be. I felt the power of the universal insight flowing through me. Friends, honestly, nothing I have ever experienced has filled me quite like this!

Fully Embodying the Presence

The day came when I remembered that the *power* is real. "My goodness, this is extraordinary!" My confidence returned. I knew that this was the lifestyle I was meant to live. How could I ever have forgotten?!

With this remembrance came a new transformation, *another* level of clarity I had never before attained. With this transformation came a spark of inner vision that surpassed anything I had ever imagined I could do. With that came an enhancement of my talents and my most joyful harvest—because I began to tap my *core* Nature in a really substantial way, which I had never before conceptualized was even possible.

When we attend to our spiritual yearnings, we magnify opportunities and draw to us all that we require to sustain our true Self's desires. In this way, I reconnected with my own soul in a more full way than ever before. I opened my total presence to the Divine through me. I can only compare this experience to the most exquisite ecstasy imaginable. The sense of devotion I felt—and still feel—is a form of rapture. The fulfillment was, and is, BLISS.

The outcome of this endeavor was writing more books than I could keep track of. Every day I was writing a chapter on one book or another. Today, I am still writing—effortlessly—nonfiction and even fiction. Books are flowing out of my spirit like water from a well that never ends. They flow from my heart and my being, just as these words are flowing to you now.

Friends, when we acknowledge and nurture the yearning in our heart, we can be everything we sense we are and have yearned to be. I can only advise you to trust the inner counsel that you hear, sense, and feel. Believe in your own power. The *guidance* is real. It is tangible, practical, and always present.

When we open our vision to our whole Perception, allowing the higher forces of life to direct us as our spirit wills us to go, our life becomes more joyful and complete in every way than we otherwise could know. Our relationships flow. We feel true affections. We are caring, impartial, unbiased, compassionate, gentle, allowing, and nonjudgmental.

In the embrace of the angels, our life is aglow with love ... and that love flows from us.

11

Attuning to the Presence of the Angels

The Two Key Universal Attitudes

When we align our energy with the different forces of being, we begin to understand the integral process of how to align with the angels. We envision the energy patterns that fill our own being. Thereby, we are able to envision energy forces other than our own. For example, we are able to see the vibrational presence of an angel as an energy form or a moving pattern of lights.

In various shapes of the light forces, the angels devote themselves to our personality's criteria for being aligned with the powers of the universe. When the angels are ready to attend to our personal needs, they reconnect us with the universal consciousness through these attitudes:

- *Surrender to life all that is holy in you.*
- *Give back to life all that you believe is holy in the world.*

How We Are All Part of a Unified Field of Energy

Once we accept that the primary function of existence is a serendipity of various conditions, we come to acknowledge, at least in our perceptions, that the natural conscious mind believes in a holy alignment of all of us together with the universal consciousness. It is by understanding the universal laws that we discern that the life forces are naturally aligned.

Therefore, when we are open mentally and psychologically to the concept of a unified field of energy, we present ourselves to the world as a portion of others. We see ourselves as connected, rather than as separate. We see ourselves as united by the very process that gives us breath and a mind by which to contemplate the nature of being. We see ourselves as friendly and open-hearted ... because we recognize that all people and all living beings are a part of the vibrational force that is our own breath.

When we integrate our inner knowing that subjects all of our previous ideas to living in harmony, we begin to synthesize the visions of our inner mind's eye with our reality of the world's experiences and our personal position in humanity. In this unique way, we surrender our attitudes of superiority to believing in a composition of life forms.

We see that all are aspects of a previously imagined fractured reality. We see that the illusions we have had were from a limited point of view, narrow in their range of comprehension and blind in their capacity to construct truisms.

This awareness unleashes itself through our inner consciousness; so that, we eliminate the various inhibitions that created confusion and dismay, due to our inability to conceptualize that reality is a living force of many aspects of a single character that is manifesting in the form of vital energies.

Therefore, when we delight, at last, in the Consciousness of which each of us is an aspect, we realize how all living beings make up this composite web of lighted forces. We see nature as a unified field of vibrating energy patterns. We comprehend the illustrious choices possible in our personal existence.

The Energy Bridge to All Higher Consciousness

When we realize the patterns that link us with all other beings, we are open to some rather phenomenal circumstances that potentially will uplevel our insight to an exquisite comprehension of all life, even life in other dimensions and other worlds. When we acquire the capability of tapping the Universal Mind, we are capable of conceptualizing mentally and esoterically all of the greater realities that are a part of this vast experience we call life.

So, we each invoke within ourselves an energy bridge to the angels who are also a part of the universal consciousness. We develop this *bridge of conscious energies* through our continuous efforts at being aware of our whole Self.

This bridge, called the antahkarana, illuminates our higher consciousness. We live in a focus of surrender to the will of the divine law that guides our every inner sense and choice about the way we exist. We release our inhibitions. We comprehend our stature as a voice of the light. We gather our energies into a singular concentration of our mental capacities. We open our mind to conceptualizing higher frequency patterns, which continuously press themselves upon us day and night; although, until we constitute this bridge of energies to the higher realms of thought, we are not able to grasp the finer sensitivity necessary to conceptualize abstractly and mentally the nature of existence. Nevertheless, this becomes not only possible but easy, once we complete the process of aligning our personality's strengths with our spiritual Identity.

Awakening to the Living Mind of God

It is said, in esoteric writings, that we come to a place in our evolutionary process that we become *"alive with the Divine Mind." This* process, described in many writings by previously noted philosophers and mystics, is often defined as *"an expression of the most extraordinary nature during which you feel touched by the hand of God."*

Such a sensitivity to the *Living Consciousness* of the life forces brings us into a sharper focus of the whole pattern within which we exist as a self. It is this pattern that becomes very clear to us as something that serves not only as an extension of our own being and mind but also as a link to other living forces and entities.

When we are able to distinguish the patterns of light around us, we are also able to visualize the various components of beings who exist simultaneously in our multidimensional reality. At this point, we can be so aware of the vibrational frequencies in the atmosphere that we are able to discern many levels of reality that co-exist with our own precious dimension.

As we become aware of these various levels of existence, essentially we *"awaken to the living mind of God."* It is this very distinctive contact with the Universal Consciousness that builds the *bridge* from our own mind to the minds of the highest plains of reality, including angels. Once we do this, we are able to receive the angels' finer frequency thought forms, as if they are standing beside us speaking words aloud. This is an extraordinary opportunity for us, because it becomes a heightened experience of *"the oneness."*

I will mention here that this process is not a substitute for an ego-desire to be acknowledged. This process only results from our continuous effort toward being aligned with all of life. We cannot possibly attain this higher synergy process without healing our own agonies, misapprehensions, and discontentments to a sufficient level of releasing them to our better Nature.

It is only when we begin to accept that even our darkness is a part of our light that we heal our wounds and let go of allowing our doubtful nature to manipulate and control our inner knowing Self.

Therefore, if we believe that angels can speak with us, we can be sure that unless we have learned to accept ourselves joyfully in all the aspects of who we are, we are more likely listening to our own ego. We learn to become aware of this process.

12

Finding the Inner Thread of Serenity

Aligning to the Greater Good

There is a place in life for every one of us. Each of us carries the insignia of God. Each of us lives our personal life in the way that will best give us the clearest understanding of how *we* are an incarnate divine being of light.

When we have been imbued with the higher awareness of angels and other illumined ascended conscious beings, we feel a strength and confidence that surpasses our previous insecurity as a personality. When we are infused with the power of our spirit, it becomes more important to us to focus on the upward striving of our psyche than to give in to uncertainty.

We reach a place in our evolutionary path where we cannot release our hold upon the higher realms; neither can we disconnect our whole presence completely, as much as we might think we do. We are so deeply attuned from the center of our consciousness that there is always at least a thread of hope, always a link in some way with our center of power.

Once we bridge the vast chasm to the higher planes of consciousness, no matter what befalls us after this, we are always able to come back with a greater ease than when we initially attained that consciousness. This can offer us now a great deal of self-assurance. For when we are troubled and distraught over an occurrence in life that seems to shatter our faith in the divine realities, we can cling with a great presence of mind to our inner place wherein we touch the power of our beliefs.

Let it be said that we *are* that *presence* when we are aligned to the greater good in our heart. The factors that distinguish the presence of light in our life is our continuous seeking of an honorable solution, our continuous hope for the finding of an amenable alternative, and our continuous constancy in our outlook for a better way of life.

It is Spirit in us that strives to the higher realms of compassionate interaction with others. Regardless of what pains us or what sorrows come to bear upon us, when we are aligned in our heart to being useful and helpful in some way, we can grasp the inner thread of serenity.

The Ways to Serenity

Let us now understand the ways in which to find serenity, if we have forgotten how:

- We kindle faith in our innate Nature, by being aware of everything we say and monitoring every nuance of our behaviors.

- When we are misaligned and we reap pain, we act assuredly and with self-confidence and we swiftly make amends.

- We do not hold back from discomfort; we confront it.

- We do not recede from challenge; we face it.

- We do not linger in sorrow or chaos; we stand clearly and depart from it.

- We do not allow the dark side of our nature to pull us under; rather, we sever the tentacles of apathy and fear.

- We dissolve in our psyche all links with pain of ridicule or rejection and we pull firmly into our light, where we stand with all the powers of the universe filling our heart with affection, compassion, understanding, humility, and self-awareness.

- If we are in error, we make amends immediately. If another is in error, we let it go and we go on our way, no longer looking backward. We live always in the highest place of our being.

- How do we do this? We raise our vision, we raise our comprehension, and we raise our perception ... through investing in ourselves via the spiritual connection.

How to Restore Spiritual Resonance

There are many ways to do this. For me, it is through a powerful meditation. When I am not able to access the connection to my spirit, I use music, the *OM,* or a recorded meditation exercise. If fifteen or thirty minutes isn't long enough to purge a feeling or action, I do whatever time is warranted to re-center, reconnect, and come back into my presence of being that is joyful, sweet, thoughtful, and kind.

These behaviors require, it seems, continuity in practice and in focus. They are learned behaviors. By the repetition of this frame of mind, and with a conscious application to it day by day, we become that person. It is possible to so release our anguish of the past and to so heal the scars of our personality that we become purified, comparatively, to all that we were before.

The angels play a very big part in this. It is they who continuously offer us their musings when we are in the midst of conflict. It is their presence pushing us to make amends and encouraging us to heal our pain and reconnect with our center, inviting us to step into the light and feel the power of compassion.

It is the angels who remind us how to live in the light of our higher Character. It is they who reach into our confusion and despair, however slight, and push us, pull us, tug at us to listen to our inner Self's counsel; to reach into our own spirit for answers and for the courage to act.

A situation may be minor, comparatively, but any kind of disconnection with another human being that causes us despair is reason enough to listen to the angels who are prompting us in our heart:

- *Rethink your pattern.*

- *Rethink your attitude.*

- *Rethink your behavior.*

- *What is wrong? Correct it. Make amends.*

- *Do not linger in self-pity. Do not linger in self-doubt. Lift yourself up now. Correct the picture.*

- *Bridge in your heart with a clear compassion for yourself.*

- *Open your being to that other person. Do not shut down. Do not pull away. That is an old behavior. That is no longer who you are.*

This impression from the angels is often unconscious and probably unspoken. It generally is subtle.

When we are confused or vague, we may feel as if there is a tug-of-war within us. When we have been in error, or accused of error, or we feel a disconnection with a loved one or a friend or any human being, we may feel inclined to pull away, withdraw, not confront the pain, not confront the other person in a gentle way.

Yet something inside of us yearns to connect, to amend, to correct our patterns, to clear the picture so we will be well again.

To Realign a Relationship, First Realign Self

For me, the quickest way to do this, the fastest response, is to go into a deeper meditation and let Spirit fill me with light—through which comes my clarity of purpose, clear sense of right action, and the courage to reach beyond my old behaviors. When in this state of being, I am able to open my heart and reconnect with the other person in honesty. I am able to bridge the vastness that may have sprung between me and the other, acknowledge my own actions and behaviors, and sincerely attempt to behave from my own highest attributes from that point forward.

Living in our light is a continuous challenge. Yet it is one that brings us equanimity and restores gratitude, which is a healing power. Such a lifestyle leads us into understanding the way life actually functions when it is in harmony.

Transcending Past Beliefs

Once we acquire insights about life's effective strategies and formulas, we are able to seriously reconstruct the way we have analyzed the nature of reality. The angels play an important role in this, because they carry the synergy of all life forces. They are, in other words, capable of reconstructing our energy patterns: physical, mental, and emotional.

This constitutes some of the criteria that lay a foundation for us to access the wisdom of the higher realms. In this capacity, we explore the farthest reaches of the universe. Once we have discerned our own place in that greater spectrum, we can more clearly appreciate the value of those beings who comprehend and transcend all that we previously thought was real.

Time spent in the study of philosophy and esoteric psychology brings within us an open mind and a willingness to explore the realms that are invisible to our perceptions here on Earth. Consequently, it is a most important realization when we begin to listen to the various theories and ancient stories about the origin and evolution of life in all its aspects; because there are many ways to describe the angels, the nature of life, and the process of human evolution. There are many ways to analyze these points of view.

The Evolution of All Life Is a Single Process

The primary form of study is through the focus of at-one-ment, because all aspects are merely threads of a whole tapestry of existence. The evolution of the angels, the evolution of life on earth and all other planets, and the evolution of humanity, are intertwined as parts of a single process—which we might define as the evolution of God. For, you see, God is the totality of all these parts. We are components of God.

When we view ourselves as part of a whole, and we see that our lives, this planet, our universe, even the angels, also are a part of that same whole, we begin to comprehend the patterns that bind us all. We begin to perceive and relate to the synergistic threads that connect us all. It is this perspective, this outline, that makes it not only desirable but possible to directly contact and communicate with those beings who are nonphysical and non-third-dimensional.

This may seem extraordinary, but it is the simplest form of truth: The angels are no less substantial in their own reality than we are in ours. They are just as imaginative, and they are delighted when we discover that our own experiences are similar to theirs.

The angels are exquisite majesties. So are we. They tell us:

May you understand yourself, but in a greater capacity than you before determined.

May you see yourself as extraordinary, and glimpse the presence of the angels.

The Angels and Humanity Are the Left and Right Hands of God

It is our viewpoint of what is natural law that opens our mind to the visions and capacity to understand the nature of the reality that creates angels. It is, therefore, not only possible and desirable to synergistically relate with these divine celestial beings; it is essential to the continued process of our spiritual and physical evolution. Why? Because we and the angels are inextricably bound in an equanimis relationship that requires our personal ability to contemplate our own magnificence in harmony with theirs.

The angels guide us, teach us, lead us, and instruct us. They are our friends and our counselors—but only until we accept our own position in the universal process and we see that each of us is equal in the eyes of God; that the angels and we are but the left and right hands of God.

We both originated in the Breath and Being of the divine forces. We both are manifestations of the Breath and Being of the Divine Consciousness. We are but different facets of the Mind of the Universal *Entity* that constitutes *everything that is.*

To be attuned with the angels, we attune to the very fabric of life itself, and we see ourselves as an integral part of that fabric. We see the whole, we see the parts, and we know that we and the angels have come from the same origin ... and are evolving individually, although together, along our own particular paths of the spiritual beings we are.

We learn from the angels who we are, what we are, where we have been, and where we are going. The angels show us the way; because they knew us when we were first created, and they will know us even in the hour when we return into the power of the Divine.

At some point in our life or soul evolution, the angels contact each of us. We cannot avoid that contact. We can only delay it.

13

Angels Helping You Find a Lost Loved One

How Is This Possible?

We are integrally connected with the vibrations of all aspects of life. We are integrally linked with all peoples, all living forms, even "inanimate" matter, because all things have an energy field of a kind. While we may not readily see these vibratory fields that exist in all dimensions, it is the natural life force pulling us together. This very decided resonance of the entire universe is called *"the essential relationship of spirit to matter."*

Sometimes we are able to integrate our own pattern of energy with that of another. Sometimes we are able to achieve a clear connection so that we feel a particular bond or relationship. When our personal energy field is aligned with the energy field of another, we are "at-one."

The synergy of our aura with that of another is the divine force evolving us. We are always evolving. Even our aura is in a constant state of development. Once we have acquired a link with the energy force of another, the energy itself is evolving. Not only do we feel different with a person, pet, or place than before, but we *are* different. The relationship is an expression of the cosmic essence and is vibrating at a level of density that uniquely expresses that singular relationship.

Sometimes this energy field is detectable; it is almost tangible. That is the *rush* we feel when we are in the presence of a person, pet, place, or object of strong attraction to us. We feel an energy field by the tingling sensation we have when something or someone enthralls us.

In addition to a very definite link to another auric field when in its presence, once a relationship is set, we are even linked when we are not in the same place. Therefore, we can find people, pets, things, and even places. How do we do that? And how do the angels engage in this process?

The synergy of auras is partly due to the angels' influence. By our attraction to the angels' vibrations, we are able to see, hear, and feel them in our lives; for angels have auras, also.

How We Are All Connected by a Web of Energy

Energy, you see, is the stuff of all existence. Energy is that essential ingredient that unites us all. It is the mesh of the life force which we all are. So, it is even possible to consciously touch and be touched by an aura, even that of our personal angels with whom we have a deep connection in the center of our spirit.

There are angels of many kinds, angels at many different levels of evolution, and angels who actually are a part of *our* eternal Character.

This latter group of angels presents our higher knowing Self's concepts, visions, and rapture; because these angels imbue us with the wisdom of their divine counsel.

In fact, the angels of our soul are so much a part of our soul's consciousness, that it is improbable that our human mind can distinguish between them. So, when we focus our attention upon our soul consciousness and enhance our link with that higher vibration, we simultaneously also are accessing the angels who personally invest us with their guidance, advice, and counsel.

It is this very special energy bond that unites us with all living things, animate and inanimate, even rocks; even rocks emit an energy field. So, when we are away from an object of our interest, we are still very much connected, by way of the cosmic "threads" to that object, whatever it may be.

This tie between us and others exists until one of us disintegrates as a conscious energy, or until we personally disintegrate the energy link itself. In other words, we can find people, pets, places, and things. We also can end our connection with them by consciously destroying the binding force that exists between us.

The Technique from the Angels
Word for word

Let us now analyze a method for attracting a person or thing back into your life. For example, let us imagine that a child is lost from you, and that you need to be aware of whether the child is alive or dead. You can still locate the child; or you can telepathically bring the child back—as long as the child is able to return and the child wills to be with you.

When a child or another person who is lost from you, and once you are sure that it is a concern, it is wise to get alone and have time apart from all distractions, so you may concentrate at the level of your inner being.

Envision

So, let me now advise that if you are struggling with the loss or disappearance of a child, or other "relationship," that you begin to consciously envision the whole presence of your child in your mental eye. Allow yourself to become fixed on that inner vision. Do not be afraid of what you might see, feel, or know. It is greater for your happiness—and the child's—to know exactly what has happened.

Intention

Use your love for the child as an impetus for beneficence rather than as a weight to help you avoid facing a potential unpleasant truth. In your love of the child, raise up your inner knowing out of your own need, into a conscious acceptance that you can understand whatever the inner vision relays to you. Separate your personal desire and fear, and focus on what is the greatest value to the child. Think not of your own need but of the very great need of your child who is less developed and experienced.

Focus

Now, with your intention clear, set yourself into an energy focus of very distinct images, feelings, and sensations. Let us picture that now.

Put away all reminders that might cause you emotional grief. You do not need the photographs or personal belongings (at this time) to make the connection solidly real to you. You need only to be still in your mind as well as to have a complete stillness around you.

Total Silence

For this, I advise, for the purpose of creating this very distinct inner resonance, that you place yourself in a state of total silence. However difficult this is for you, it is necessary. You can only truly perceive the child's face and aura if you are separate from your grief. The stillness of the environment will help you begin to feel the stillness inside of you.

At first, this may not be easy. Of course, you will have pain—and that is okay; it is a healthy way to heal. However, for the purpose of having the child well or returned to you, you do need to relinquish your grief; set it aside for now.

Be aware not of your own need, but that your entire attention to the child's well-being is what will save him or her from any unnecessary struggles beyond what already may have transpired.

Choose a Place

Now, choose a physical place where you will be able to sit in silence. This can be anywhere; although the child's natural environment is a stronger access to his or her energy, such as the room in which he or she sleeps or spends a lot of time.

Put away (for now) mental images of what might have happened to your child. This is not the time to investigate the cause or sequence of events. For this exercise, you want only to focus on seeing, perceiving, or sensing your child's aura. Nothing else.

Time Alone in Contemplation

Once you have decided on a suitable place for this technique of the inner vision, make arrangements with the people, who otherwise would be present, to leave you alone for a while to "pray" or "contemplate." If you cannot tell them what you are planning to do, just tell them that you need to be alone for a while to think and to get yourself in order.

Out of courtesy, most people will understand that you want to be alone. If they do not and they insist that you be in a certain place or do a certain thing, do not argue; do not invest emotional energy into being able to create the place for the attunement.

If you must, even say that you just need some silence for a while, to be left alone, such as to take a long hot bath. In whatever way you can peaceably arrange it, without emotionally investing yourself or activating any kind of a "scene," arrange the privacy you need to be alone "with your thoughts."

A Quiet Hour

If you are unpracticed at meditation, you may require more than one session to get into this feeling. If you do meditate, or at least regularly practice "alone time," give yourself an hour to get into the connection and to "pick up" whatever you can at that time.

I will mention that it will be easier for you to do this technique when you are rested; when the mind is rested, there is less potential for mentally getting off the focus. So, an excellent time to find a quiet hour is during the night. You may arrange the time in advance if you wish, to attune while others are sleeping. You also may be available to attune at any time during the night when you spontaneously awaken; it is easier to concentrate when you first awaken.

Before Eating

Let us assume then that you have selected a place and decided on a time that will offer you an environment conducive to this exercise. You now need to prepare yourself physically. It is easier to focus *before* any food is taken, not after. If you try this exercise after eating, there will be less blood in the brain ... and you need all of your energy focused in the mind. So, delay eating until *after* you have made this connection.

Delay Stimulants and Depressants

Also, if you smoke, delay smoking until after the hour (approximate), until after the session is complete. Of course—for this hour—no alcohol, sweets, stimulants, or drugs that would impair your thinking process. In other words, be able to concentrate astutely; delay any outer stimulants or depressants that may affect your ability to concentrate.

Now You Are Sitting in the Room

Now that you have dealt with the physical and begun to put your emotional needs aside (for now), let us imagine that you are sitting in the room where you will be doing the visualization. Let us imagine that you are in the child's bedroom in the middle of the night. You have just awakened. You have taken a few moments to ready yourself so that you are physically comfortable. You have had a drink of water and relieved yourself at the toilet. You are neither too cold nor too warm. Everyone is asleep, and you have already discussed this plan so you will not be interrupted.

Now you are sitting in the middle of the room, either on the floor or in a chair. You have a blanket around you if you need it. All lights are out, except for perhaps the dim glow of a night light. All photographs are face down. There are no visual distractions.

After reading these instructions, close your eyes (at least partly).

Deep Breathing

Begin to inhale deeply, counting to ten and slowly releasing. Inhale through your nose, pause, and release through your mouth. Do this for several minutes.

Deep breathing serves several purposes. It balances your aura, stills your mind, centralizes your focus, calms your emotions, and increases your vibration to a higher conscious frequency so it will be easier for you to access the consciousness of your child.

- Breathe deeply, slowly, and calmly. Breathe in and out in a rhythmic motion.

- Allow your breath to follow its own rhythm. Be with the breath.

- Totally immerse yourself in the breath. Become one with the breath.

- Become the breath's rhythm. Flow in and out with the breath. In and out, in and out. Flowing, still, and calm.

The Mental Screen in Your Mind's Eye

All of your thoughts now merge into a single focus, not by your will but by your natural attraction to the intention you already have set.

In the calming rhythm of your breath, now centralize all of your attention on your inner eye. Feel your mind clearing. Feel your total attention completely, coherently, and distinctly concentrating on *only one thought:* Looking at the mental screen in your mind's eye.

- See the screen. (It may be white or black, but it is a solid color and there is nothing else around it.)

- Now see the screen dissolve and, with your inner eye, see a void.

- In that void, there is nothing but complete darkness.

- Place your attention visually to that void. See it. Be aware of it.

- Into that void, visualize (calmly) the presence of your child appearing. (You do not need to observe details for this to work. You need only to have a vague sense of your child's presence.)

- Visualize your child's aura, the light around him or her that vibrates outward from the body. Imagine it.

- Now be still and relax. Let go of your emotions, release them. Focus (for now) only on your goal: to be at-one with your child in your inner eye. (This is the time of greatest clarity. You may see a picture, or you may only sense it. Either way, you will feel a presence distinctly. For these minutes, you are definitely aware of your child's energy or presence in your mind's eye.)

- Now begin to more consciously see your *own* aura. Perceive your aura vibrating out from you as a living force.

- See also your child's aura, and see it fluctuating.

- Allow the sense of the two auras to become real to you, visually. Be very aware of this. Continue to breathe regularly but calmly.

- Now allow the picture in your mind's eye to become crystal clear. Whatever you see, feel, sense, or just know, make a mental note to yourself … but continue. (Do not stop. You will remember.)

Creating the Safety Field

Now that you have picked up whatever information is apparent, you can begin to consciously *place* your child in a vacuum of energy, a force-field that works like a safety net.

(Remember, all things are energy. All things are composed of energy, even mind. Mental energy can be directed; it can be shaped and defined. Mental energy manifests, in the form of an etheric force, whatever is focused and visualized in the mind's eye.)

- *Now envision a bubble of* **white light** completely around your child. See that light as a shield through which nothing but good can penetrate. Make that shield of light solid in your mind's eye.

- Reinforce it now with *a bubble of* **blue light**. The blue bubble surrounds the white bubble, and both surround your child. See the blue light as solidly real. Both of these lights form a force-field of protection around your child against any outside force that might cause harm. (The energy fields of these two bubbles is electromagnetic. It vibrates at a frequency that repels, unconsciously, whatever intentions are not in the child's best interest. The unconscious dissonance of the energy fields to any potentially harmful intention or circumstance actually alters the way in which that other person or object or situation interacts. In other words, remember, all things are connected by a web of energy. When a focus sets the energy into a vacuum [or bubble] that intends to ward off all energies that do not represent the highest good; in a sense, a force-field is generated. Whether or not you accept or understand this, release any personal objections. Flow with the image, create it ... and trust in the power of mind.)

- Now that you have placed your child inside the vacuum of the protective force-field, pause. Breathe slowly again and re-stabilize.

- Now become aware of *a solid band of the white light energy directly linking between your center* (solar plexus, center of the ribcage between the breasts) *and your child's center.* Observe this band of solid white light between you. Feel it, sense it, know it.

- If you do not see it, just have a very clear awareness of it. If you do not perceive that this band does solidly link you and your child together, it may be that your child is no longer alive (in the body).

- Breathe deeply now. Slow down your thoughts. Get calm. You need to complete this process. You need to know for sure, and you still need to release your emotional attachment. Regardless of whether your child's consciousness is still in the body, your child is still conscious and does need your help. So, either way, set aside your own desire and emotion. Lift yourself back up into your mind's eye and the clear objectivity of spiritual discernment.

- See the bubble of white light around you. Visualize your child with you *inside* this bubble of light.

- See you and your child both inside this bubble of white light. Again, observe whether it is so. Is your child definitely with you in the mental picture? Do you *feel* it?

- *Embrace your child.* Have a very real sense of your child's presence. *Trust what you know.* Accept what insight comes to you now. Be with it. Let it soak in.

- Be still now, just be still. Breathe slowly.

- Allow the calmness to fill you and to smooth out all of your feelings. Be in the embrace of the light.

- You will have received very clear impressions of your child. Trust this and let it go now.

Believe and know that your child is not alone. Know that your child's angels are with him or her. The angels are real; they do exist. Although they do not always intervene, because of our own higher purposes, they do remain with the consciousness of every person, whether in the body or not.

Let us assume that your child is alive. Let us assume that you also sense this, even that you have relieved your concern by strongly perceiving and sensing the *"cosmic umbilical cord"* of white light between you, even that you easily envisioned both your child and yourself together in the same bubble of light. Trust this awareness.

At the same time, do not emotionally attach to it. Just accept that, in the highest probability, the circumstance is exactly as you have perceived and sensed it.

What More Can You Do?

Once you have generated the protective bubble around your child and sensed whether there is still a physical connection, now turn to the angels.

Open your heart and mind and let their energy imbue you with their goodwill, love, and compassion. Let their splendid and exquisite energy become the force that heals you and offers support.

Open your whole being to the angels. Call to them. Ask for them:

"Be with my child. Help him (or her). Protect him."

Call upon all the angels to assist you and your child. Ask for their intervention:

"... in whatever way you can be there, in whatever way you can help."

Turn over your control to your spirit within you. Let the spiritual you be the one who acts now. Listen to and act upon whatever spiritual insights come to you now.

This is the time to pray, to totally release the outcome to the divine Source. It does not matter by what names you call God or the angels. Now is the time to ask for their help and intervention:

"... in whatever way it can be offered."

Trust the Divine Source

Let go now. Know that you have done all you can. You have mentally attuned. You have spiritually connected. You have done and are doing physically whatever can be done. Now let go. Release to God—to the Universe, the All That Is—whatever outcome is in your child's highest good:

"I have done all that I can. I can do no more.

"It is my wish to have my child returned to me—safe and well, if that is at all possible—but I release all that I will, and I ask that the Universe make clear to me what is in the highest good.

"If it is possible that my child be returned to me, let it be so NOW. If not, then I ask for understanding."

Release and let go. Allow the angels to work the Law for you. They will. They do. They are.

Heal Your Child's Uncertainty by Remaining Calm

In the event that you realize, or later discover, that your child is no longer in the body, remember that your child still needed you. With this awareness, know that the energy bond between souls does not die. Our consciousness does not die. Your child is still very much aware as a self. You can still help your child.

Yes, you need to grieve—for the loss of your child in your physical life; but allow that, in time, you can release that. For now, dwell not so much on your loss ... as on the *energy* of your child.

Whether or not your child is conscious in the body or out of the body, these steps of spiritual alignment are still necessary. In fact, if your child is no longer in the body, you can heal your child's fear by remaining calm and centered in your spirit; and it is still vital that you ask the angels to assist:

"Be with my child. Guide him (or her). If possible, bring him back to me safely—and soon. If not, then go with my child and ease his way in the new life."

So, bringing your child home results not from your personal detection of where your child is, but by releasing control emotionally.

When you have done this technique and been able to allow the angels to help you, you might find insights coming into your awareness. If you do, then certainly follow up on them. But if you do not, trust that in some other way the process of reestablishing a physical connection is now happening.

I know this may be difficult for you to believe, but I have had several personal experiences with this. I have been amazed more than once at how the "universe" functions.

We are all connected. The energy does tie us all together. I trust this information, and I offer it to you with a blessing for your peace of mind and contentment.

Let go, my friend. Trust that the angels are with your child, and they are with you.

14

The Possible Holy State of Being

Remembering Your Original Self

In this age of transforming beliefs, let us consider the possibility that, as you recall your original state of being, you become more able to live in a presence of mind that is always holy.

I must admit that this is an ultimate challenge. However, I am sure, from my inner knowing Self, that if I continue to reap such anticipation with hope and commitment to the higher realms of thought and being, the day indeed will manifest when I—as the rest of humanity—will ascend into a perspective and action of character that is resolved toward being holy at all times.

I imagine this takes a lot of practice. But who knows, perhaps the angels are right. We do see around us in the world some few examples of this, people who—at least to our perception—appear to have acquired the demeanor of angels;

people who, compared to the rest of us, have assumed the temperament of angels. Two examples are Mother Theresa and the Dalia Lama. There must be others.

Such people give us a point of view about how to live in our truth. We can learn from such people what is possible as a human being. I imagine that the possibilities are endless. Let us, therefore, analyze the complexities of one who is evolving into the angelic state of reason.

How We Know When We Are Evolving Into an Angelic State of Being

- We care not only for our self but mostly for the well-being of the whole. We care for all.

- We do not demand attention, nor feel the need to be heard for our great intellect.

- We search daily for ways to apprise ourselves of knowledge and wisdom of the ancient ways of perfect harmony in our state of life.

- We characterize ourselves as illuminating the very character we are each day.

- We live in harmony with all life forms, regardless of how we perceive their existence.

These are a few qualities we develop in our character when reaching a higher level of existence and consciousness. Let us, therefore, be grateful that such qualities *are* attainable while in the body.

Where Humanity Is Headed Now

In the very near future, comparatively, humanity will be very much in alignment with these concepts. Today, it seems impossible; but it comes to me as a pungent fragrance of the Divine that *undoubtedly this is the very certain direction in which we are headed.* The day, indeed, will come when this state of consciousness will be the "norm." (It is our privilege, therefore, to hold this vision that humanity someday will acquire a state of presence that is a very much finer quality than ever imagined before for our species.)

Is there anything we can do to hurry our process toward this Utopia? I don't think we can hurry any faster than we are. *We may seem to be stagnating, but we are not.*

The undercurrent of change is awakening our hearts to a greater compassion. Our minds are expanding to a greater intellect. Our personalities are undergoing massive changes in our perceptions of what is valuable. Our bodies, even, are becoming inured with wholesome strains of devotion to wellness.

It is very clear to my Insightful Self that we, as a whole, are moving toward self-realization. We are leaping beyond known territory—psychologically and culturally.

The typical transition of a species is not dimensional, as it is now. The day will come, no matter how much we resist it or deny it, that humanity will evolve into a very clearly devoted presence of angelic nature. The world we care about is a manifestation of that same frequency of love. Therefore, for us to change the world, we must first change ourselves.

Once we each realize that humanity is an extension of all our selves, and that each of us reflects the trend in which humanity is evolving in sensitivity, we then comprehend how important it is to realize our own innate angelic nature. Let us, therefore, contemplate what we can do individually toward achieving this presence of mind and being.

How We Become this Evolving Self

- The *first step* is to self-heal our pains of the past. Acknowledging the discordant qualities in our personality (which we are able to perceive and release through therapeutic treatments of our character) enables us to see our potential inner Self and identify who we truly are. As we peel away the layers of doubt, fear, anger, confusion and self-denial, we become more and more assured of our loving disposition, more refined and sympathetic.

- As we resolve our personality issues and gain energy of all kinds—mental, physical, emotional—we move on to the *second level of self-realization;* which is to clearly acknowledge the potential of our power. As we pass the various stages of self-doubt and become more certain of our innate nature, we grasp, along the way, the nuances of what that power is.

- Strength of character is not forced by will. Strength of character is the result of loving ourselves in all of the various aspects of who we are. We are multi-faceted beings with much to gloriously embrace.

- Our beauty far surpasses what few discrepancies remain in our psyche. We lift up the light of our inner peace, which engulfs us ... and tranquility seeks us as completely as our breath.

- When we devote ourselves to being whole in all that we are, and we forgive all of our mistakes, we begin to claim the divine *Presence* in us; which is the power with which we were all created and is our inner knowing Self.

- Once we begin to claim our power in harmony, we move on to the *third stage* of the self-discovery process and acquire an intuition about life and the greater spectrum of experiences that lie before all of humanity. We reach a level of sensitivity to the greater whole.

- With this comes a responsibility; because it requires an enormous degree of compassion, integrity, honor, synchronicity, and a balanced disposition. We must have learned the various stages of self-awareness and integrated our own higher consciousness. This is an enormous task but with bountiful rewards and joy.

Our inner Self loves responsibility. It is our innate Nature to give and to be the total Self we are.

Let us each open our heart now to exploring the vast possibilities that lie before us, wherein we can remember our origin and we shall blossom.

It is with hope and true humility that we evolve into our higher conscious Self, aligned in light and in love.

15

We Are All in an Evolution of Consciousness

Why and How Angels Were the First Beings

We humans often consider ourselves as ultimate entities of the Divine. We forget that not only are we not the last word in species, but that the angels were created before humans came to be. Therefore, we can learn about ourselves from the angels, because they preceded us on the scale of evolved entities.

Then Came Humans

Let us imagine the first time humans existed. It was our hope that the differences between celestial and terrestrial realms would be for our edification. It wasn't long, however, before those who became human learned that the struggles far surpassed the advantages. However, by this time, so much already had happened to our personalities and energy frequencies that it was not possible to merely return to our previous state of being. We, therefore, recycled ourselves in order to renew our original "voices" in sweetness and in joy.

The most significant and telling indicator of a person who is ready to return into the level of angelic consciousness is an inclination to be absorbed by angels and all of that mystery. This does not mean that person will immediately pass over. However, it does indicate that the individual is preparing for the final stages of life's adventure. It does mean that the cycle of rebirths is approaching a conclusion and that the current incarnation may very well be that person's last as a human being.

As we approach living the spiritual life, let us remember what the purpose was for our becoming human in the first place. We desired to explore reality and to investigate options available for realizing our natural quiescent Nature. We also felt drawn by curiosity to investigate many different kinds of realities. In those cases, the beings who did this did not remain human or did not choose only the human form.

For those of us who did, we realized that the human form is a great deal like our higher form in constitution; except, of course, for the differences of density and manifestation, which are quite distinct and visible when compared to our original being. Aside from the characteristics of our physical body, the similarities between humans and angels are vast.

How Humans Are Similar to the Angels

Let us now focus on those similarities and, thereby, what we humans can hope to comprehend of our own true Nature. At first, we may not recognize ourselves in this description. However, it is definitely who we are when we are totally at-one with our true Nature. Therefore, this will help us to see what areas in our personality need correcting; because as we dissolve our personality dysfunctions, more and more we align to our divine Nature—which is our *natural* state.

We begin by considering why angels exist, which also tells us something about ourselves. Angels came to be as a result of the Universal Consciousness desiring companionship, someone to hear Its voice, to see Its light, to comprehend Its furthest extension of being, and to share in Its reality as Consciousness.

The angels, foremost, are divine examples of most pure thought forms. They represent a hierarchy of various realms of expertise. Through their numerous functions, they supplementarily provide, to all species, a program of anticipation of clarity and at-one-ment with the Consciousness as a fortunate state of being.

Us, By Comparison

When we see ourselves in comparison to the angels, we often admonish who we are. Yet, indeed, we are descended from those beings. When we decided with eagerness to explore the many different degrees of vibration, we became enthralled with the experiences we currently know in physical reality.

When we first became enamored with this process of physical manifestation, we did not realize the inherent difficulties. However, we soon came to see that this degree of the vibration has a price. Cloaked within the lower focus of the Divine, we became numb to our inherent divinity. Over time, we forgot that the *link* is natural and inherent in us.

Always we have strived to reconnect with the splendor we once knew. We have honored that *splendor* in the moments we have seen it, felt it, and touched it. Yet because we have come to miscomprehend the *bond* between us and all that is holy, we see that *splendor* as outside of ourselves.

And Now?

Now we are awakening. Our world is vastly changing. While we may not understand these changes, let us remember that it is a natural process of the evolution of consciousness.

The earth and humanity are in the throes of transformation. We are reaching up into a higher level of our being, pulling ourselves forward against the tide of the life vibration here—because we have come to see and know that there lies within us something greater than we have known. We are beginning to tap our Spark, our eternal Flame.

It always was within us, but we did not before accept that it is a part of us. More and more, however, we are realizing that the Divine—to whom we give all of our allegiance—is more truly *within* us and manifesting outward. We see the beauty of life around us and we are in awe. However, we may just as well remember that the beauty is within us, because we are exquisite examples of the consciousness of God.

The Angels Reflect Our Inherent Capacity

So, the angels reflect our capacity. They are present in numerous forms and in numerous ways, coming in waves of indescribable bliss to remind us of our inherent capacity so that we may feel the *presence* of the Divine (not by the angels externally imposing themselves upon us). When we feel their energy, it moves through us, penetrates us, and sparks to life our own vastness of the Divine—from which we came.

Each of us is exemplary in all respects. The angels are present—in increasing numbers—to remind us of what we once more can be. The similarities between us and the angels far surpass the differences.

- We both care about each other.

- We both live for the purpose of becoming more than we have been.

- We both reach our most stable and centered Character through our commitment in service.

- We both relinquish wholeheartedly those facets of the universe that are remnants of a blind society called the Nefilim. We are no longer the ones who dropped out of the light in search of our own vain glories. We have had time enough to restore the balance of our *godselves.*

Awakening to Bliss

We are now awakening in our hearts; and, belying all superstitions, an eagerness is pulling us yearningly forward into an extraordinary bliss:

- Once we accept that our inherent Character is holy, our behaviors change and we become as an angel walking upon the earth—because our entire focus for being becomes to be of service to all of life.

- We develop a sensory perception of the functions of every being. We gain an insight into the interconnectedness of all living things. We gain an appreciation of our own place in the spectrum of all experience.

- With our new senses and devotions, we learn to compromise. We learn to blend and to be a part of the whole, to share ourselves in harmony and in balance.

- We learn to cultivate a clarity and synchronicity of purpose that is for the good of all. No longer do we live in fear or uncertainty. We are raptured daily by the sureness of our inner knowing Self.

This Is Who We Are

Those qualities are already present in us, waiting only to be released. That happens as we face the blemishes and spots on our character grown from the misuse of the power as an unknowing self.

When we were children, we did not know, we did not understand. But we are no longer children. We have come of age. And with us are the angels guiding our way, along the path of self-realization as beings who honor all.

Let us, therefore, reanalyze ourselves. Let us see that we are indeed capable of communicating with the realms of angels; that, indeed, they do communicate with us.

Each one of us carries the same composition of traits. The angels are not unlike us, even though they are holy divine beings who maintained their link with the pureness of Spirit. When we reattain that degree of at-one-ment with *our* own holiness as our central attribute, we rekindle the Person that we are, which at one time was an angel.

When we each first evolved out of the I AM's embrace, into becoming human, that was but one element of our life process. In the beginning, we were born *attuned* to the spectrum of divinity we call angels.

Angels are the forerunners of our human society. They are our predecessors esoterically. They are currently communicating with us more actively than ever before, so we may tap into the spark of life that we carry in our own being.

By the angels' very presence, we are reminded of who we are … and what we can be. They are the reflection of our true inner Self.

Revealed Teachings

Appendices

The Futurist interview

July 9, 2012, World Future Society
www.wfs.org/futurist-interviews
Associate editor Rick Docksai interviewed
Charol Messenger, futurist and spiritual author:

People today don't just have more technology than their ancestors; they actually have more intelligence and a heightened sense of right and wrong. Just ask the neuroscientists who have documented an increase of more than 10 points in the average adult's cognition since the 1980s; as well as the Flynn Effect, a rise in global IQ scores since the 1940s. They're not entirely sure why these mental advancements are occurring, but they vouch that our brains are fundamentally higher-functioning than those of any generation that preceded us.

As for our ethics, Harvard psychologist Steven Pinker and Tulane University political scientist Christopher Fettweis both authored books in which they note declines in warfare and violence worldwide over the last century, and reasons to believe that the world will become steadily more peaceful in decades ahead. You can see THE FUTURIST's reviews of both books— Pinkers' *The Better Angels of Our Nature: Why Violence Has Declined;* and Fettweis' *Dangerous Times?: The International Politics of Great Power Peace.*

Recently, THE FUTURIST associate editor Rick Docksai spoke with another voice of hope for progress, the futurist and spiritual author Charol Messenger. In *Humanity 2.0: The Transcension,* Messenger describes a new evolutionary stage for the human species that she says is now under way: Communication networks are flourishing, cultural barriers are breaking down, and individuals everywhere are attaining new levels of empathy, insight, and awareness. She shared her thoughts with Docksai in this interview.

THE FUTURIST: You speak of an "evolution" that the human race has always been undergoing. This evolution is making a major "leap forward" this century. As you describe, it's a mental, spiritual, and physical evolution. How does the physical evolution manifest itself?

MESSENGER: Humanity's physical evolution is the awakening of existing genetic strands.[4] This exhibits itself in an increased ability to perceive complexities, and a sharper aptitude for intuitive reasoning. These characteristics result in a faster ability of mental processing. Some indicators are higher creativity, more sensitive intuitively, and a clearer comprehension of subtleties. Examples of this are the people whose grasp of the finer realities is heightened; as in scientists who extrapolate scenarios based on conjecture rather than known results, and scientists whose ability to conceptualize new eventualities far reaches beyond previous thinking.

THE FUTURIST: IQ scores have been rising worldwide over the last century, according to researchers, who call it the Flynn Effect. To what degree might this be a sign of human evolution?

---

4 All four of my uses of the DNA term "strand" were received during my 2011-2012 escalated receptivity, as I was highly keyed in to the coming December 2012 winter solstice, with the pervasive news about the Mayan prophecy — and was getting my own perception of all that.

MESSENGER: The universal effect of a physical evolution in the human being is most evident in the capacity of the "faster brain." We are in flux. We are not who we were. And we will continue to accelerate by every new generation. The long-range effect of this is an increasing ability to see the whole. We gradually begin to understand how "all are one."

THE FUTURIST: Some would say that the social media revolution is a human consciousness shift—people all over the world can interact, exchange ideas, and be connected like never before possible. What role might Facebook, Twitter, and the like play in our evolution?

MESSENGER: The new technologies are one means by which all humanity begins to reach across the great gulfs between people and join common causes. The greatest benefit of this is community. We begin to draw together, to really feel how all peoples are parts of some greater whole. There are complications. Not everyone is thoughtful. But the true shift in global consciousness is like a tsunami, and it is rolling through societies like a flood wave. It will continue and cannot be stopped.

THE FUTURIST: On p. 167, you describe a cultural values shift taking place in the Middle East, and it includes growing affirmation of children's welfare and respect for women. What examples can we see of this?

MESSENGER: The world is still filled with unconscionable acts toward women and children. What is new is an increasing demand for justice. Women and children themselves are speaking out and leading this new soft revolution globally. The new movement to safeguard children and women has breath now, and it will only grow—in much the same way as a wildfire rages across a land by only a small breath upon it.

THE FUTURIST: You describe an "energetic resonance," an energy field of Earth that has been accelerating in recent decades and positively affecting human evolution. This makes me think of the Global Coherence Initiative, in which engineers created a Global Coherence Monitoring System to track fluctuations in the Earth's magnetic field and ionosphere. The system found that not only do the magnetic fields change right before certain natural disasters, but that people's moods, heart rates, and thought processes change along with them. And, according to the Web site: 'There is also evidence of a global effect when large numbers of people create similar outgoing waves.' Perhaps it's charting the same energy field that you are writing about. To what extent is Earth's energetic resonance measurable? And to what extent can we interact with it?

MESSENGER: Basically, all of the topics discussed here are interrelated, not distinguishable. Already you can see the incredible effects of a faster brain, the most tangible evidence of an evolving human being. Secondly, as the human mind is expanding in its cognitive abilities—evident in increasing empathy—the planet is dynamically altering in its magnetic frequency. The rate of one's vibratory resonance or frequency is the primary indicator of the level of intuition (there are levels, or degrees) and the level of dimensional existence. The more resonant you are to higher thought (fast mind), the more you are able to embody empathy and to exacerbate intelligent intervention in solving the world's problems. Bottom line, the Resonance Factor affects all living things.

THE FUTURIST: You write that a new spiritual consciousness is unfolding across the Earth. What is the future of the world's religious traditions and creeds?

MESSENGER: The human race takes millennia to evolve. This includes changes in cultural practices. Structure was needed for survival. One form this took was organizations in all forms. Most people turned their lives over to people who did seem to have a more substantial comprehension of the great puzzle called life. However, now all of that is shifting. For this century, religions and dogma continue. Yet the number of people awakening to a personal connection to the inner divinity is the main observable event. The new spirituality is without structure. It is in the self. Religions, dogmas, creeds will disintegrate, in time, for the greater whole. The new spirituality is personal. It may be sharing. There may be groups. But there is no dogma. No one dictates required behaviors. The awakened self learns that the grace of personal humility is all the guidance one needs.

The new spirituality is individuals discovering that the true value of our lives is in how we open our hearts, how we treat each other, and how we are without judgment. As we, as a people, learn these qualities, that is the degree of our spiritual evolution.

World Future Society, 7910 Woodmont Avenue, Suite 450, Bethesda, Maryland 20814 301-656-8274

The Request

In a deep meditation, my oversoul spoke into my heart-mind and said, "My name is Samuel."

I saw him in a dream one quiet afternoon in Colorado during a short nap. I looked up and this very handsome man in his forties walked toward me, dressed in a modest, brown monk's robe with a hood. He came to me like a father. He came to me as a friend. He came without grandeur, but with a clear and steady gentleness. And I knew: This is one called Oversoul. This one is the source of my being. This one is the purpose of my life, and I am to teach his message:

> Be who we are, now, today. And fear not. For the true divinity, the wisdom, the strength, the guidance, is not an outer force or magic—but is us ourselves.

> *We* are the ones who create our life, our reality, our joy, our sorrow. *We* are the ones with the power to change it.

> The Divine Light is in us all, without exception. We find that light when we pause in our busy lives—and allow the breath of life to carry us into the womb of creation … where we were born and always will exist.

> We of the world, we and all around us, are part of one Living Consciousness. And it is good. And so are we.

Meeting Oversoul in a Vision

March 5, 1982 during seven-planet alignment

A delicate fragrance of rose potpourri filled my quiet room. I curled beneath my periwinkle-blue afghan and gazed out the bay window at the prisms of afternoon snow filling the crisp Colorado air, floating down softly and blanketing the earth white. The resonant dancing lights reached into my soul and embraced me.

Alive. I am. Forever.

In that moment, I could see beyond all boundaries, through all, and familiar thoughts streamed into my mind:

Be still. Be still and know that God is in you. Be still.

This mantra into my mind soothed me, calmed me, stroked away my fears.

Be still. Be still and know that God is in you. Be still.

Drowsiness overcame me and I drifted into a light nap, wherein I saw an iridescent figure. The familiar light-being took my hand, and warmth flowed through me. We lifted beyond this world to a very bright hall and stood before a large double door. It opened and we entered a lovely garden of flowers, with singing birds and flowing fountains.

The light-being departed and a tall, ageless, spiritual master walked toward me. His stride implied an inner strength born from much experience. Yet he came without grandeur, with a clear and steady gentleness. His brown hair and beard complemented his modest, brown priest's robe with a hood, of the ancient archetypal order of Melchizedek.

This handsome man, looking to be in his forties, came to me like a father. He came to me as a friend. His deep, brown eyes revealed a quiet and mellow nature.

"My name is Samuel," he said.

He took my hand and we strolled through the garden, as he explained that in one lifetime he had been known as the prophet Samuel in the biblical Old Testament. After many lifetimes and inner explorations, he had grown beyond the boundaries of external reality and the struggles of human life. No longer bound to a body, he had ascended as his true Self into the timeless realms as one of the Unseen, now neither masculine nor feminine.

That was when he remembered he was an oversoul—*my* oversoul, the being from whom I first came to exist as an independent personality.

Until age thirty, I had journeyed throughout my life without consciously knowing of my oversoul's existence. Yet Samuel had guided me. His feelings had impressed me; and his thoughts had reached into my deepest self, embodying the soul presence into my life.

Samuel and I now came to a room of mirrors. "Why have you come?" he asked me.

"I want to know," I answered humbly.

"What do you want to know?"

"Whatever you will show me."

We walked through the room, looking at my own many reflections of different incarnations, and Samuel said of other Ascended Masters, angels, and himself, "We have little more knowing than you, but we have come far since physical life. Perhaps our insights and understanding will help you and your friends find an easier way."

"What can I do?" I asked.

"Give. That is all we ask. Let others know that life is not coming to any end. Let them know that they are each a divine aspect of the universal life force. Let them know that beings exist who respect and love them and offer support on request. Let them know all that we will tell you. Be our messenger. Let us teach through you."

We returned to the garden and, as Samuel departed, a tall slender woman with long midnight-black hair approached me. She gazed at me warmly with love and affection, and a reverence fell over me. Alexandra was the other half of me, my "twin flame," who also originally had come from the same oversoul; then she and I had decided to explore different kinds of reality as separate selves.

"My gift," she said, "is to give you all you have known and to lift you up. Prepare yourself, my friend. Join me now."

We walked and I listened and learned, transcending into expanded visions and hope.

"Indeed," said Alexandra, "there is always hope."

She and I planned the rest of my current life and I came to remember what I had known before about the realms of limitless thought.

We then traversed the universes and I brought back memories of these sojourns, which I share in this and many other books. "Embrace all, be all," said Alexandra. "Know that your dreams are already fulfilled, even as you give yourself to them."

The Angels Today

Those today we call angels are divine beings of Light who never incarnated into physical reality. Elements of *What Is,* they remained in the *Realm of Always.* Their primary duties are to serve and assist humanity. They are perfect and clear Light, forever in harmony with all. They do not set themselves above any, and they take responsibility for human guidance.

For the Messenger books, they have opened the scroll from the esoteric Hall of Records on "Humanity's Origin" and they say to us, "We are your ancestors, humanity. We are your brethren. You were once here in the realms of *The Before Time.* This is how we know you, love you, understand you."

The highest of the highest of the orders of angels are called the *Angels of Serendipity,* as written in the Hall of Records, whose name represents their essential quality and character.

They are the first angel clan in the Universal I AM, the first beings created. They oversee the ever-changing Akashic Records, which contain *all* experience, *all* knowledge, and all events that are yet unfolding.[5]

Angels of Serendipity are the *Watchers of the Light* and the *Keepers of Wisdom,* which denotes those who herald the Light, present the Light, foster the Light, and are protectors of the Light.

As the Keepers of Wisdom, they are caretakers of the Word. The Word is *inner speaking.* The Word is the *First Cause* expressed. The Word is *The Divine* manifest. They are the *Keepers of the Word* because they are the nearest to the Source Mind.

---

5 To know the four angels who help you every day, read my book *Wings of Light,* given from the angels.

The Seven Speaking to Humanity

I was wakened out of a deep sleep at 4:40 a.m. May 7, 2011 with these words in my mind:

This is the I AM. I have a message.

I got up, went to my meditation room, and wrote down these words as they came into my mind, phrase by phrase:

"This is the I AM. Humanity, we in Life's Purpose hear you.

"Who are we that speak in the familiar language of soul through this teacher? We are Soul. We are Presence. The seven light sources that speak are in the direct line of the Alice Bailey tradition. We are the line of Melchizedek, the monastic Order of Knowledge. We are the revealers of Life's Purpose. We are seven, in service to all humanity and all life.

"Our purpose is clarity. Our purpose is teaching the inner way. We are seven of the soul of this teacher, whose being is tempered to the realms of the Divine Presence; whose life force is immersed in bringing insight regarding all the events shaping a new transcending and sweeping, lasting reinventing of the human nature.

"We are known as angels. The Divine is all. Our words are in the language of the Divine. We bear that Fullness as a lamp, to show what is coming. We speak from the fire of creation, which is ongoing and never ending. We cannot hold up any who fears. We are through with fear. We are now bringing words to fuel a true knowledge:

"Life is always. Life is never ending. Life is the wherewithal to hear simplicity. Life is not drudgery. In your own center is the answer to *all* questions.

"It is our task, with this teacher, to show the energy thoughts underpinning this world. It is our task, with this teacher, to focus why these new pressures are pushing out all old faded delusions of Purpose. It is our task, with this teacher, to heal the uncertainty and to foster a more true Picture of what is in store for all in this world.

"We of this teacher's tempered light now open the doorway to Earth's evolution. This is not the end. Time does not end. Humanity does not end. Nature is not ended. Earth is now, already, vibrating to a pitch that cannot be stopped or avoided. All is now moving Purpose up to a view of the possible.

"Your being is light. You are *light.* The one truth is: All life is this essential element. Light is life. It is the visible Identity. It is an eternal driving power. It is your own vision, inside you. Inside your mind, light is the illumination, a magnetic essential component … of all that lives. Illumination is life, its nature.

"Why do we say this now, we seven of the soul of this teacher? Because all you have thought is now *expanding.* Nothing will be as it was. All of the fears are only a need to see. See what? Your own inner essence—which is boundless illumination, unlimited ability to imagine, incredible cognizance to know all around you. Believe it. It is real.

"The I AM Presence (speaking) is the Fullness of this teacher. This teacher is tempered in these four attributes:

Listen to your knowing that guides you.

Live with the attitude that every being is the divine in body.

Open your mind to greater things than ever imagined before ... and they will become.

Live in hope ... because hope is the Divine guiding you.

"This teacher is of The Old Ones and is our human representative, conveying our words and ideas. With this teacher, we are able to help all of humanity begin to come out of the long slumber.

"We seven *are* the I AM life force. We serve only the good. We are the ancestors of this teacher. We are those who live to serve the Divine.

"Breathe...

"All is the Divine. All is in the Wisdom. And so it is."

From The Seven, September 15, 2011:

"We seven are from the Divine Alliance called the Angels of Serendipity.[6] It is our task, through this teacher, to share Insight— because humanity is awakening. The human race, on Earth and elsewhere, is now in its new strain.

"This is your time. You have awaited the Origin's arrival. You have anticipated the King's presence. You have requested the personal Elevation to touch you. You have held in your hopes that God is a pure and good Overseer.

"God is not an entity. God is the Presence of *All That Is,* that which is the vibrant essential quality that constructs elements, that called the Original Matter and the Quintessential Organic Substance and also the very qualities *From Which life* gestates.

"So, we seven are original Selves out of the Conscious

---

6 For more on this, read appendix "The Angels Today."

Expansion. We have been since *The Thought* expanded out of the Essential Vortex.

"Now we can consciously tell you: You also came out of *The Thought,* and your new life is the example you have breathed in order to re-find your Original Definition.

"*Know this:* As a human, you are the example of *The Thought,* which sent Itself out To Be. You, now, are escalating … through enhanced neuro links. You, now, can hear Thought guide you, teach you, and even heal you.

"We are the reminders. We remind you of who you are. We remind you how to hear us. We are all of The *Thought.* You, too, have essential Supporters who guide you back to remembering. Your life is, now, about to expand—so that *your* voice is heard.

"Life is a place to be fully all that you are, in the serenity that is you. Invite that serenity. Tap it. Live it. It is *your* essential Self."

April 13, 2012 at the end of that morning's meditation:

I was expressing gratitude to the Source of these writings for the nurturing energy, when this inner response came to me:

"We are your Soul Council, seven who assist in this global awakening of all humanity, to help ease this first-ever shift into the physical dimension called *Full Presence.* It is our way of contributing to the whole, reminding everyone that *all* peoples have this same gift. It is who we all are. Everyone is able to access the *Full Mind."*

Messages from Oversoul

Soul Essence of Charol Messenger

Each person has a unique vibration from the beginning of his or her eternal existence. Our soul name identifies our unique essence and represents the essence of our higher self and the highest good of our personality. Our soul name is not the name of our oversoul from which we extended, nor the name of our physical self.

"I, Calantra, am but a humble servant of Yahovah, the one, the all life, the light, the Essence, that of which I am. I am given wisdom to perceive most completely my path and each step. I am given assistance in those things that I must do. This is indeed an honor. I feel the power as it moves me and as I am taken in it. This power is most substantial and grand indeed.

"My God, the light of love, is my only speaker. The Yahovah who moves in me is my light. And the Christ is my companion, at all times present and ready for me to receive its spirit. As I do, I am in wonderment at the words given through me, for I know that they are true. I seek no other path but the I AM's in all that I do.

"I am an emissary from Elijah, who has instructed me with numerous manuscripts that are being recorded and transcribed by my physical aspect [Charol Messenger]. I, Calantra, am an emissary from Perona.

"I am one of many incarnate spiritual teachers sent from Elijah to Earth to make ready the race of humankind by raising the consciousness of the planet. We invite those who are moving upward in expanded awareness and who live by example the wisdom of the ancient masters, who teach not by bending heads but by being whole."

Oversoul Samuel

One's *oversoul* (aka overself) is the first aspect extended from the I AM of that self; and disperses into many aspects as personalities through time, space, and assorted dimensions for a full flavor of spiritual evolution. Each personality grasps different experiences and develops a particular gift or attitude, all of which go back into the Whole. We may be predominantly male or female throughout our many personalities in various lives/incarnations, in different times and places in the histories of planets and other dimensions.

Charol Messenger's oversoul:

He has given me the name *Samuel* to relate to *him/her* based on his significant previous earth incarnation as Samuel the Prophet in the biblical Old Testament. Following is Samuel's own description of his being and life as that prophet.

"I, Samuel, am the oversoul and master teacher to Calantra, the soul [universal essence] name of my physical aspect Charol Messenger. Calantra, the extension of my being in your time and space, is one of my many selves. Through her I teach and counsel many.

"I, too, am merely one on the path. Although I have recently entered the sixth level of existence [of seven], I, too, am still striving to comprehend my full potential. I am blessed with the presence of the angels. I also am blessed with a master teacher

158

who is near fulfillment [Djwhal Khul]. He has instructed me to give guidance in these days of new beginning on planet Earth.

"Some have called me prophet. But I am merely a messenger of the Yahovah—the I AM—as many are. I am greatly honored to have the opportunity to make available these lessons given to me from my master in the Christ realm, the seventh level. These lessons are taken from the sacred scrolls of the Angels of Serendipity, who are the highest of the highest of those created by The First Essence manifested from The Life Force.

"The council and I join together to present to you, through Calantra, the understanding that the angels have given to us. We are not giving instruction only because we desire to, but because we have received direct guidance from the I AM to do so. And as we speak to you, so you may speak to others.

"I had an incarnation as a prophet described in your Old Testament. My body of that lifetime was called Samuel. I was raised in the orthodox manner of the time and became a priest. That self raised in consciousness when *my* being as an **overself** extended to the personality, in the same manner in which I now communicate through Calantra. Calantra and I are aspects of one Self.

"That Old Testament incarnation was not my first existence. It was only one aspect of my being. My whole self is evolved beyond the one called 'Samuel, the Prophet.' I am more than that body. However, the name Samuel is in harmony with my present purpose through Calantra, the current physical extension of my being.

"Of the seven levels of existence, I have just recently entered the sixth. While I am far from perfect, I do have more vision than my channel Calantra, who is one particle of my essence who chose to reach out, learn, and experience. Although Calantra is my self extended, throughout this work she also represents her own identity and personality. At the same time, she is representing my identity as Yahovah's holy speaker."

For additional information about Samuel, his story is found in the biblical Old Testament, books Samuel I and Samuel II. Also see the archives of Edgar Cayce, considered the foremost psychic and prophet of the twentieth century; his health diagnoses are world renown for their remarkable accuracy for thousands of people.

In addition, references are made in three volumes by Robert W. Krajenke based on Edgar Cayce's story of the Old Testament: *A Million Years to the Promised Land* (Genesis through Deuteronomy), *Man Crowned King: The Divine Drama Unfolds* (Joshua to Solomon), and *Man the Messiah: God's Plan Fulfilled* (the kings, prophets, and rebuilders). Briefly, these accounts (which I did not read until December 1999 in preparation for publishing the first edition of *The New Humanity*) indicate that Samuel:

> "was an unusual and highly developed soul who appeared at a critical and difficult stage in Israel's spiritual development.... During their transition ... Samuel received direct guidance.... [He] was the last judge of Israel and the first of the great oral prophets.... [He] established a School of Prophets based upon the teachings of Melchizedek.... He was priest, judge, and prophet [and held] a unique position in Jewish history.... Samuel is seen by many commentators as a spiritual foreshadowing of Jesus Christ who represent[ed] the final fusing of priest and king.... [At] a critical and crucial time in Israel's development ... [Samuel's

leadership and prophecies affected] the history and the destiny of [a] nation"

... and today the world, through many of his speakers on Earth, among many such Counselors and Prophets who bring new hope to the world and new light to the value of seeking to live the spiritual life (Krajenke, Robert W., *Man Crowned King: The Divine Drama Unfolds*, pp. 94-95, NY: Bantam Books, February 1974).

In *Man the Messiah: God's Plan Fulfilled*, Krajenke reports that Elijah gave Samuel's School of Prophets its greatest impetus. The school "was turning out individuals familiar with higher states of consciousness and knowledgeable.... The prophets knew how to 'tune in' and receive from God" (Krajenke, Robert W., p. 113. NY: Bantam Books, September 1974).

Messenger's Soul Councils

We are responsible for our own actions. No one designates what we must do. Our spiritual teachers and guides merely show us a path, a direction to make our way through life less troublesome. They and the angels guide us through dreams, meditations, and promptings through our inner guide.

Charol Messenger's primary soul council:

"Friends of Earth, you and we are not so different. It is only a slip in time and space that seems to separate us. We are all a part of one another. We are all a part of the Great Oversoul [God]. As we [each] truly begin to comprehend this, that is when our life transforms. That is when we begin to live the miracle and nothing is beyond us.

"We, the council of Calantra, are the *Watchers of the Light.*

We are the *Keepers of Wisdom.* There are several councils to this channel, in descending order of authority. Each council has seven beings of varying responsibilities. The oversoul, Samuel, oversees us all.

"We, as a council, are one of an infinite number of such councils. In all ways and all places we represent the angels, the servants of our Lord Yahovah—the one Light, the All, the Essence that gave us being. As representatives, we are instructed to give direction to our physical counterparts. We assist those who do not yet perceive their spiritual nature. Our work is of the soul.

"A council is what we do, not what we are. We the council of Calantra are instructors. We are not yet perfect. We, too, are evolving along a path of higher wisdom. The instructions given through this book were handed down to us from masters, from angels, and from the I AM—in that order.

"We, the council, are followers of Christ Consciousness [divine essence], believers in spirituality, and pathfinders in new ways of understanding old truths. We worship the I AM, All That Is, Yahovah; and we are ancestors of Calantra. We have wisdoms that have been passed down from the Angels of Serendipity. The information in these books is not our own; we have been allowed to share it with you. We are reading our translation of the angels' text, which is originally in the form of symbols. We give insights only on that which is our expertise.

"You may wonder about the information in these books. We are not trying to replace what has been given previously by other visionaries, mystics, channels, and philosophers. We merely wish to embellish the Earth record for a greater understanding. The content in these books is distinct from other writings and ages because of the variation in theme and the times in which wisdom is received. Otherwise, the patterns of evolution are similar and identifiable as a basic philosophy of existence.

"What we present here is a philosophy, a way of perceiving life and a soul's interaction with life. We are offering a program for ample success at being and for achieving peace of mind while in the body. We have no expectations of what you get from these books, except that you grow in your own awareness. Yours is the final truth. We are grateful for an opportunity to share with you our vision.

"You hear within yourself The Source. The ideas in these books are our perception of reality. If, with an open heart and open mind, you explore this new dimension of your being with a full recipient will, you will discover insights that transform your way of being. You will learn that *you* are the master of your fate, and that there are angels to guide and help you. May you find serenity."

Messenger's primary soul council: Oversoul Samuel, Gadeah, Zodeah, Josiah, Leshun, Joshua, and Suzanne.

Oversoul Samuel is a recognized authority of the fifth level of existence, having only recently entered the sixth [of seven]. He has mastered many of the obstacles and obstructions of the previous degrees of reality.

Joshua is Charol's protector. He is an archangel, of the blue ray, under service to Archangel Michael. (Soul is blue ray, also.)

Leshun and Suzanne are guides.

Gadeah and Zodeah are Angels of Serendipity. They never incarnated. Gadeah is a masculine vibration and the equal counterpart of Zodeah. They both also are part of the original spark of the soul (e.g., overself/oversoul) and parts of the origin of that which is now Calantra (Charol Messenger). Zodeah is a feminine vibration, pure consciousness, the highest vibration manifest, a christed being, perfect and holy without the slightest dimming of light:

"We have come to guide [humanity's] hand. We are instruments of vision. You see within you our countenance and our splendor as we sit on the council of Samuel, for Calantra. We are here, real beings existing. We are real, but we are not the same as you, [not] in concrete form. We are Angels of Serendipity, in perfect harmony with the Creator and with The Force That Is."

[In 1982, these two angels "sent" "The Principles of Balanced Being," published in *Visions of Serendipity,* an early version of *Angels of Serendipity* (in production), a few select pages in spiral binding for workshop participants and a few close friends; now being published in its entirety. These same ten new Universal Laws were later "re-received" spontaneously in 1994 for *The Soul Path,* in different words but the same concepts and in the same order, written in plain English for our modern times and retitled the "Tenets of Clear Being." The comparison chart of both versions are published in *The New Humans: Second Genesis* and *Intuition for Every Day.*]

Josiah is a master teacher, fourth dimension incarnate, not on Earth, a high order individual. Soul commended him to Calantra's service to remedy a past disservice to her. Mending has taken place. There are times when one may choose to work through other dimensions of consciousness to give assistance:

"I have been a compatriot of Calantra. I am 'a wonderer and a sacrificer.' I am not the jewel of patience. But I do have great sight."

A shared past life with Josiah: "I, Josiah of the hills of

Samuraiso in the early days of the conquest of Latin origin the concubine, was an authority over Calantra. There was a great antipathy between us. I was a powerful mongerer. I was wicked and unbelieving of things taught about humanity's true nature. I threw Calantra away to service as a slave. Long did she not forgive me. Lives later we were still at war. I grew concerned with Calantra's continued antipathy for me. It was given to me to assist her in this lifetime. I dedicate my time for this period of evolution to give her strong support, to offer strength.

"One more word. I Josiah am not a fragment of universal mind. I am not an aspect of Calantra's higher self. I am not a projection of her subconscious. I am myself."

Along with Oversoul Samuel and Alexandra, Josiah is a "sender" of the text in *The New Humans: Second Genesis, 1982 portions,* on how time and matter manifest in fourth-dimension physical reality.

Messenger's secondary soul council *includes* Alexandra, Charol's writing partner.

Both Alexandra and Charol (Calantra) are part of the same oversoul, both from the same *original spark* of soul.

During the first physical existence of any humans, they were one being, as an incarnated Angel of Serendipity.[7] They were among the first physical human incarnations, on a now-nonexistent planet, Perona, in the Pleiades. This first human incarnation experience is relayed in *The Memory* (in revision).

In their second lifetime, Alexandra and Calantra reincarnated as separate physical beings, thus "twin flames," on different worlds.

---

7 For more on the Angels of Serendipity, read the Introduction.

Alexandra is currently a higher-dimensional being. In addition to being the *muse* behind all of the Messenger books, she wrote *You 2.0* volume one on Higher Self initiation and integration (original title "The Daily Routine of a Developing Initiate"); and in *The New Humans: Second Genesis,* the chapters on mind and its functions, fourth-dimension consciousness, and the fourth-dimension human body (the latter, written with Josiah). Alexandra says to all readers:

"Do not look on us teachers and the angels as gods, unless you see yourself also as a god. We give our names only so that you may realize there are dimensions other than the third and planets other than Earth with intelligent life, some physical and many nonphysical.

"We teachers and councils all work together. We of the councils have feelings and needs, as you [of humanity] do. Each of us also is learning and becoming more aware and complete in remembering our true Selves. You and we are all a part of What Is. You and we are all one breath and one body.

"We do not encourage you to seek *our* personal counsel. You have your own helpers. We encourage you to open your heart to them. Whether or not you are aware of their names, you can seek their assistance. As you become more aware of your own guidance, you will gain a clearer understanding of your daily choices in life and the path before you.

"This is a book for growing and learning and remembering that you are God."

More About the Author

Charol Messenger spontaneously awakened to the universal consciousness at two a.m. November 2, 1975. As a result of this mystical activation, she has the spiritual gifts of clearly hearing, discerning, and interpreting the language of the soul—the "language of light."

Charol is a translator of esoteric knowledge and the etheric Akashic Records into human language in practical, everyday terms. All of the phases of her spiritual development that followed the awakening came upon her unbidden consciously and without any preparation or training; nevertheless, each phase was a part of the greater Soul Plan for this incarnation.

Carrying the signature and blueprint of her oversoul—the biblical prophet Samuel—Charol "elected" to be born in July 1945, between VE Day and VJ Day at the end of World War II, to be part of the upcoming transformative social changes on planet Earth.

In the fall of 1975, Charol encountered a life-threatening situation over several weeks. During highly charged and shattering encounters with dark spirits, she faced the "dark night of the soul." Latent psychic abilities and spiritual sight flooded to the surface of her consciousness, saving her physical life and her sanity. Thrust into dire circumstances and bombarded in her mind by images and tauntings by demons, she turned to prayer for the first time in fifteen years and asked God for guidance and protection. With the wisdom and strength of an old soul, she stood against the forces of darkness, stubbornly standing in the light and refusing to give in.

At the culmination of this "long dark night of the soul," Charol saw and heard the chorus of angels in heaven, and their ethereal light illuminated her bedroom during an *overlighting* by her oversoul consciousness. The outcome of this ordeal was the beginning of merging that higher consciousness into the physical body, mind, and personality.

This "soul merge," known esoterically as the Third Initiation, took six-and-a-half years to fully integrate. From five days before, through five days after March 5, 1982 (the day of a seven-planet alignment), this oversoul integration completed spontaneously, evidenced by eleven days of continuous heightened awareness and euphoria during which the oversoul consciousness fully embodied.

Two months later, in May, Charol was wakened out of a deep sleep by a gentle inner voice speaking *into* her mind, the voice of an angel on her soul council. This was the beginning of a writing phase during which Charol received, through inner dictation, several books from the oversoul consciousness on the spiritual path, the history and origin of the angels and how they help humanity, and our evolving human society. Charol received these books one at a time, taking dictation from the clear inner voice between the hours of two and four a.m., when she was wakened out of a deep sleep each night by an inner prodding. As she heard each word or phrase, she repeated it into a tape recorder. For the next twelve years, Charol transcribed, light edited, and integrated the information at a deep level of the Self. She did not publish these works; she only shared portions of the early pages with workshop participants as handouts, and with close friends.[8]

---

8 In addition to oversoul, senders of the 1982 portions of this book on how time and matter manifest in fourth-dimension physical reality were Alexandra and Josiah on Charol's soul council (described in *Wings of Light* and *You 2.0*). Alexandra also wrote the 1982 portions on mind and its functions regarding fourth-dimension consciousness and the fourth-dimension human body. Alexandra is part of Charol's same oversoul, from the same *original* spark of soul, and is currently a higher-dimensional being. Alexandra and Charol's first incarnation is relayed

Then in 1994 another spontaneous event occurred during a six-month 24/7 period of exalted consciousness that resulted from very deep and prolonged meditative states, two hours at a time, daily. Having left a full-time job in April, Charol spent 100 percent of her time committed to renewing the connection with her spiritual Self, and she thrived on the rejuvenation.

After seven weeks, during an especially deep meditation, Charol *lifted* to a place in higher consciousness she had never reached before (and didn't know she could, had not sought it nor expected it). Writing from this new pristine place within the soul—the most pure place one can reach and bring back the insights into the world—Charol wrote five new books within four months. She spent all of her waking hours transcribing (and absorbing) the inner-dictated materials; which, interestingly, she now received in her own point of view as if she had sat down and written them, including the anecdotes about her own life, which she had never before consciously realized.

Into these five books from the Higher Mind, the same essential ideas and topics were conveyed as had been received twelve years previously, except now in new words and with flawless writing: the angels in our everyday lives *(Wings of Light* and *Walking with Angels)*, the spiritual path and our eternal soul journey *(The Soul Path)*, humanity's first incarnation *(The Memory)*, and the origins and evolution of humanity *(The New Humanity,* 1st Ed., which is Vol. I in the 2012 updated and expanded *Humanity 2.0;* the original *New Humanity* concept draft

---

in *The Memory* (in revision). In addition to being the *muse* behind all of the Messenger books, Alexandra wrote *You 2.0* vol. I on Higher Self initiation and integration (workshop handout in 1987 was titled "The Daily Routine of a Developing Initiate"). (Other early pages handed out were "Higher Consciousness Workbook" the early development of the completed *Intuition for Every Day* and "Visions of Serendipity" the early draft of soon-to-be-published *Angels of Serendipity.)*

was received in 1982, then re-received spontaneously in 1994, as you see it).

The revelations, mystical knowledge, and prophecies in all of these books are written in the Higher Mind, through the oversoul consciousness. All of the books are published verbatim as received, word for word; except for light editing, renaming and rearranging some chapters, and adding subheadings.

As a futurist and global visionary, awakened to cosmic consciousness and her oversoul in 1975, then the I AM Consciousness in 1994, Charol is a *spiritual revealer,* attuned to the undercurrent hum sweeping through humanity today. She is revealing humanity's long foretold evolutionary transformation—that is happening *right now.*

Humanity is in *transcension.* We are in it, now.

Recommended
Movies, Books, Audio, Video

First, I highly recommend *Networked Intelligence (Vernetzte Intelligenz)* by von Grazyna Fosar and Franz Bludorf, published 2001 in German, www.fosar-bludorf.com.

The following excerpt opens the discussion on how science is identifying greater capacities of the brain, including what have been considered extraordinary abilities, such as clairvoyance and telepathy—which I believe are innate within all human beings and will be evidenced more and more as humanity's evolutionary leap continues:

"New research suggests that human DNA is a virtual biological Internet and superior in many aspects to the artificial one. Could the latest Russian scientific findings help to explain the phenomena such as clairvoyance, intuition, spontaneous and remote acts of healing, self-healing, affirmation techniques, unusual light, auras, spiritual masters, the mind's influence on weather patterns, and much more? The answer may be yes.... Only 10% of our DNA is being used for building proteins.... The other 90% has been called 'junk DNA.'"

I also highly recommend:

2017 movie, *A Dog's Purpose,* based on the book *A Dog's Way Home* by w. Bruce Cameron

2016 movie, Marvel's *Dr. Strange*

In addition:

Hands of Light, Barbara Ann Brennan

Vision, Ken Carey, Harper San Francisco

Mastery Through Accomplishment, Hazrat Inayat Khan

Freedom in Exile: The Autobiography of the Dalai Lama

Surfing the Himalayas, Frederick Lenz

The Seat of the Soul, Gary Zukav

Living with Joy, Sanaya Roman

The Possible Human, Jean Houston

The Cultural Creatives, Paul H. Ray

Initiation, Elizabeth Haich

The Sacred Journey: You and Your Higher Self, Lazaris

Space-Time and Beyond, Toben and Wolf

Illusions, Jonathan Livingston Seagull, Richard Bach

The Education of Oversoul Seven, Jane Roberts

Psychic Self-Defense and Well-Being, Melita Denning and Osborne Phillips

The Impersonal Life, DeVorss & Co., Publishers

Life and Teaching of the Masters of the Far East, Baird T. Spalding

The Celestine Prophecy, James Redfield, Warner Books

"Getting in the Gap," Wayne Dyer

Pathways to Mastership, audio set, Jonathan Parker; Gateways Institute

"Chakra Balancing and Energizing" audio, Dick Sutphen

Joseph Campbell videos on mythology

I have not read the following books, so as not to influence my own writings, but I recommend them based on their topics, for a broad view of what visionaries are sharing.

The Third Millennium, Ken Carey, Harper San Francisco

The Power of Now, The New Earth, Eckhart Tolle

Bashar: Blueprint for change, Darryl Anka, New Solutions Publishing

New Cells, New Bodies, New Life! Virginia Essene, S.E.E. Publishing

You Are Becoming a Galactic Human, Virginia Essene and Sheldon Nidle

Angels are our forebears. We are their descendants, returning. With us in this journey of our reawakening, through all our toils and strifes, are the angels—at our sides, our befrienders, our guides.

This book is a portrait of their aid to us. It also is a portrait of our journey into being divine. How magnificent we have been. How magnificent yet!

Although our sojourn seems craggy for endless miles through myriad and distant shores, there is a lightbearer showing us the way, whispering in our ear and guiding our heart. Surely such mysteries of which dreams are made and stories woven are a truer glimpse of who we are and the life we lead?

If we could but glimpse the essence of our light, would we grieve so heavily and forlornly for lack of wisdom? Perhaps a wise one is s/he who rests in the sure knowing that unseen hands guide us, that we are offered self-reflection as a tool for our trek, and hope its mentor.

Little comes to those who have no heart for reaching. Only when we reach do we grasp the hand before us; only when in our solace—when we release our woes and all pretenses—can we fathom those beings previously unknown to us, who walk in our dreams and mists of mind.

Surely these beings are of God? What other measure do we have than the love we feel in our bosom? How else can we know the Divine than by the peace brought to us? When in the arms of grace, is that not Heaven? Can anything so gentle be less?

Angels are the enlightened ones, our counselors. We know them by their gifts to us: gentle humor, touching grace, simple honesty—never adorning us with promises of gold or grandeur, which are *our* dreams.

Blessed are we who know them as they know us.

Made in the USA
Columbia, SC
17 July 2017